PAPAL PRIMACY
AND THE
EPISCOPATE

PAPAL PRIMACY
AND THE
EPISCOPATE

TOWARDS A RELATIONAL
UNDERSTANDING

MICHAEL J. BUCKLEY S.J.

A Crossroad Herder Book
The Crossroad Publishing Company
New York

The Crossroad Publishing Company
370 Lexington Avenue, New York, NY 10017

Printed in the United States of America

Library of Congress Cataloging-in-Publication Data
Buckley, Michael J.
    Papal primacy and the episcopate : towards a relational
understanding / Michael J. Buckley.
      p.   cm.
    "A Crossroad Herder book."
    Includes bibliographical references (p.).
    ISBN 0-8245-1745-8 (pbk.)
    1. Popes – Primacy. 2. Catholic Church – Bishops. 3. Catholic
Church – Government. I. Title.
BX1805.B83 1998
262′.13 – dc21   97-45932
                                              CIP

1 2 3 4 5 6 7 8 9 10   02 01 00 99 98

To

PATRICIA

and

FLETCHER

*in loving memory
and in the sure hope
of the resurrection*

Father,
into your hands
we commend our brother and sister.
We are confident that with all who have died in Christ
they will be raised to life on the last day
and live with Christ
forever.

— *Funeral Liturgy, The First Station*

In order that the episcopate itself would be one and undivided
and that, by means of a close union among the priests,
the whole multitude of believers should be maintained
in the unity of faith and communion,
He set blessed Peter over the rest of the apostles
and instituted in him a permanent principle of both unities
and their visible foundation.

Ut vero episcopatus ipse unus et indivisus esset,
et per cohaerentes sibi invicem sacerdotes
credentium multitudo universa
in fidei et communionis unitate conservaretur,
beatum Petrum ceteris Apostolis praeponens
in ipso instituit perpetuum utriusque unitatis principium
ac visibile fundamentum.

— Prologue, *Pastor aeternus,* Vatican Council I

Contents

Acknowledgments

As this book goes to press, its author should pause over the gratitude he owes to others, a debt he would gladly pay:

To Joseph Cardinal Ratzinger, prefect of the Congregation for the Doctrine of the Faith, for his gracious invitation to participate in the symposium sponsored by the Congregation on the "primacy of the successor of Peter";

To Archbishop Tarcisio Bertone, S.D.B., secretary to the Congregation for the Doctrine of the Faith, for his unfailing kindness and facilitation of the symposium in its innumerable details;

To my colleagues in the department of theology at Boston College for their discussion of an earlier draft of the monograph that is now this small book;

To Joseph Komonchak, Peter Hünermann, and Clifford Kossel, S.J., for their review of the several drafts of the document and their suggestions for its betterment.

To the members of the doctoral seminar at Boston College on primacy and episcopate for the analysis, interpretation, and arguments that occupied many hours of the Wednesday afternoons of the fall of 1996;

To Francis A. Sullivan, S.J., and Michael Himes for their insightful and collaborative direction of this doctoral seminar that provided the context in which this book was written;

And above all, to my two generous research assistants, Joseph Curran and Brian Hughes, for their hours of scholarly digging in libraries together with their unflagging, competent help in the completion of this work.

Four Dimensions of the Question

The Problem

The original version of this essay was a response to an invitation from the Congregation for the Doctrine of the Faith. The Congregation was planning for December of 1996 a symposium that would consider the nature of papal leadership in the Church. Among the studies requested for this symposium, Cardinal Ratzinger, the prefect of the Congregation, asked for one on the relationship between the primacy and the episcopate, a doctrinal study that would be preceded during the symposium by two historical studies.

The task that was to engage this essay, then, was a modest but intimidating one: in something of a doctrinal synthesis (1) to identify some of the essential and indispensable elements of the Catholic faith regarding the relationship between the primacy and the episcopate, and (2) to delineate some of the doctrinal elements which today would merit further study. The second part of this mandate might give one pause. Surely, one would think, there is no element of this massive subject that does not merit further study. But the adverb "today" indicates the purport of the phrase, suggesting those variable settlements that bear with particular importance and urgency upon the reflection of the contemporary Church. The essay should presuppose rather than repeat or extend the historical studies of the past century as well as those composed for the symposium itself. It was to be both doctrinal and synthetic, its initial title given as "Doctrinal Synthesis: The Primacy and the Episcopate."

One should note as precisely as possible the task to be undertaken: it is not to discuss the primacy; it is not to discuss the episcopate. It is to explore the relationship between them, an exploration that will bear upon the primacy and the episcopate as the component units within this relationship: what are its indispensable elements, what are dispensable and consequently open to change? The essay is not a historical study, an examination of the evolution of concepts, claims, and practices, but it relies heavily for its reflections and arguments upon the historical studies of others.

William Henn, O.F.M Cap., in his splendid historical overview of this subject for the second millennium did not add to the comfort of the task when he stated that "the more adequate harmonization of primacy and episcopacy, of the church universal and the local church, is widely considered to be *one of the most pressing theological tasks of the Church today.*" And what he stated as proposition, he had put even more directly as question: "Can papal primacy be conceived in such a way that it does not derogate from the proper dignity and ministry of the bishops, either taken singly or as a college? Can the authority of bishops be understood in such a way that it does not essentially compromise the fullness of authority which is necessary to an effective ministry of primacy?"[1] However one understands such vexed terms as "Church universal" and "local church," these are not questions one answers; they are questions to which one responds — with greater or lesser degrees of inad-

---

1. William Henn, O.F.M. Cap., "Historical-Theological Synthesis of the Relation between Primacy and Episcopacy during the Second Millennium," *Il primato del successore de Pietro: Atti del simposio teologico, Roma, dicembre 1996* (Vatican City: Libreria Editrice Vaticana, 1997), 219–20, 215; emphasis added.

equacy. In any case, they provide a target towards which one should aim.

The importance of this issue and of the task of this essay was underlined by Paul VI in his allocution to the Secretariat for Promoting Christian Unity on April 28, 1967: "The pope, as we well know, is undoubtedly the gravest obstacle in the path of ecumenism. What shall we say? Should we call once more upon titles which justify our mission? Should we once more attempt to present it in its exact terms such as it is really intended to be — an indispensable source of truth, charity, and unity?"[2] The paradox of this problematic situation should become clearer as the argument of this essay progresses.

Besides determining the character and importance of the question, a word should be said about "doctrinal synthesis." A synthesis is not a summary. A doctrinal synthesis is not a list that reviews and presents all the individual judgments and doctrines that a particular subject matter admits. The character of synthesis lies in uniting under one concept a divergence of facts, arguments, and propositions — things, thoughts, and words. At the end of his essay, William Henn summarized what the Church had come to teach officially over the second millennium. Since this official doctrine will be presupposed as supplying the components for a doctrinal synthesis, Henn's conclusions may be cited here:

> Official doctrine . . . has affirmed the divine origin both of the primacy and of the episcopacy within the Church. It has rejected any radical opposition between the two. It has asserted that the college of bishops needs a head to serve as principle of unity and of coordination. It has taught that the primacy is rooted in the personal promise to Peter and to his successors so that they might serve the collective unity of the episco-

---

2. For the entire text, see *Documentation Catholique* 64 (1967): 870; *AAS* 59:7 (June 28, 1967): 498.

pacy and of the whole Church. It has proposed as necessary to such personal primacy the freedom to effectively foster the unity of the Church as a whole, in such a way that this freedom is not legally conditioned by the approval of the episcopacy. It has affirmed that the primacy is bound to respect and collaborate with the episcopacy, which is also divinely established by Christ for the well-being of the Church. It has taught that both the college of bishops, as a whole together with their head, and the primate as head, have an obligation and right to care for the unity of the Church as a whole. It has affirmed the sacramentality of the episcopacy and thereby the dignity of each individual bishop as a vicar of Christ in such a way that the primacy does not and cannot diminish that dignity. It has proposed that the primacy and the episcopacy are bound together by ties of hierarchical communion.

[On the other hand] It has not explained precisely how all of these principles function together.[3]

It is this latter situation that elicits theological attempts at a doctrinal synthesis. To ask for a doctrinal synthesis of the relationship between the primacy and episcopate is to respect explicitly something of the nature of human knowledge. As Michael Polanyi has argued, the human intellect comes to meaning as it brings elements and experiences, random facts and theories into "a focal awareness of a whole."[4] Knowledge consists in bringing a multitude under a unity; the many are understood in terms of the one. The elements that carry this multiplicity, then, become parts of a whole, constituents brought into their unity or intelligibility by a governing vision that gives them context and a particular significance. To attempt such a synthesis is, consequently, to inquire into the whole, the governing concept, in which other constituents of

---

3. Henn, "Historical-Theological Synthesis," 263.
4. Michael Polanyi, *Personal Knowledge: Towards a Post-Critical Philosophy* (New York: Harper and Row, 1962), 57–58.

the total teaching will find their pertinent intelligibility and validity. This will be the attempt of the following pages.

For there must be a way for theologians, in their service to the Church, so to understand the relationship between these great realities of the primacy and the episcopate within the mystery of the Church that the claim of *Pastor aeternus* can be advanced as prescriptively realizable and as descriptively accurate: " ... this same [power of the bishops] is asserted, strengthened and defended by the supreme and universal pastor, according to that statement of Saint Gregory the Great: 'My honor is the honor of the universal Church. My honor is the steadfast strength of my brethren. Then have I been truly honored, when it is not denied to a single one to whom it is due.' "[5]

---

5. The Latin text and English translation of the decrees of the ecumenical councils are taken from the *Decrees of the Ecumenical Councils*, ed. Norman P. Tanner, S.J. (Washington, D.C.: Georgetown University Press, 1990). Reference is also supplied to edition thirty-five of the *Enchiridion symbolorum, definitionum et declarationum de rebus fidei et morum*, ed. Henry Denzinger and Adolf Schönmetzer (Freiburg: Herder, 1973). An ET of many of these documents that has been consulted is that of J. Neuner and J. Dupuis, *The Christian Faith in the Doctrinal Documents of the Catholic* Church (New York: Alba House, 1981), to which the translation of the epigraph at the beginning of this essay is particularly indebted.

The text cited above reads in its original: "Eadem [potestas episcoporum] a supremo et universali pastore asseratur, roboretur ac vindicetur, secundum illud sancti Gregorii Magni: 'Meus honor est honor universalis Ecclesiae. Meus honor est fratrum meorum solidus vigor. Tum ego vere honoratus sum, cum singulis quibusque honor debitus non negatur' " (*Pastor aeternus*, chap. 3 [DS 3061]; Tanner, *Decrees*, 2:814 [m]). The citation from Gregory the Great is taken from his *Letter to Eulogius of Alexandria*, VIII 29 (30), *Monumenta Germaniae Historica*, Ep. 2, 31/28–30; PL 77:933C. The same claim is made in *Lumen gentium*, no. 27: "Eorum [Episcoporum] itaque potestas a suprema et universali potestate non eliditur, sed e contra asseritur, roboratur et vindicatur, Spiritu sancto constitutam a Christo domino in sua ecclesia regiminis formam indefectibiliter servante"; "Therefore their power is not destroyed by the supreme and universal power, but on the contrary it is affirmed, strengthened, and

Language

The difficulties of this topic lie not only with the massive character of the problem, but also with obscurities posed by an often indeterminate or misconstrued terminology. In some cases, vocabulary has become almost impossibly elastic. J. Michael Miller suggests that part of the solution to the ecumenical problems about the primacy of the pope lies with a reform in terminology: "A precise terminology can clarify, if not totally resolve, many of the problems which arise in a theology of the papacy."[6] But this is far more easily honored in the enunciation than in practice. Joseph Komonchak notes, for example, that the two dimensions of the Church — universality and individuation — are described in various terms, and that "the Second Vatican Council did not use a consistent vocabulary for either dimension."[7]

As the meaning of the language is sometimes confused, so also is its referent. Was one not encouraged to expect from such a phrase as "from the institution of Christ the Lord or by divine law"[8] a historic choice and act of Jesus, while now it is expanded to include the providential direction of the Church by the Holy Spirit?[9] Should one distinguish "Petrine function" or "Petrine ministry" from "papacy," if only not

---

vindicated by it, since the Holy Spirit unfailingly preserves the form of government established in His Church by Christ the Lord" (Tanner, *Decrees*, 2:871).

6. J. Michael Miller, *What Are They Saying about Papal Primacy?* (New York: Paulist Press, 1983), 86.

7. Joseph A. Komonchak, "The Local Church and the Church Catholic: The Contemporary Theological Problematic," *The Jurist* 52 (1992): 416.

8. "ex ipsius Christi Domini institutione seu iure divino."

9. *Pastor aeternus,* chap. 2 (DS 3058); Tanner, *Decrees,* 2:813 (m).

to cloud what is essential to the former with the legacy of scandal and fury that have accrued to the historical dimensions of the latter? There is no satisfactory solution to this dimension of the task. The language bears too much historical weight to permit easy understanding. It might be useful at least to raise the touchy question of the relation between conciliar statements about primatial power and of often-taken-for-granted social theology underlying them. This matter, of course, has been thoroughly investigated by Herman Pottmeyer and supports the maxim that one cannot presume a continuity of concept or philosophy in an identity of language.[10]

Even the term "primacy" is systematically ambiguous. "Primacy" was applied to or recognized in a particular see or a particular bishop, as this term was referred to the forms of primacy recognized by Nicea in the three initial patriarchal sees of Alexandria, Rome, and Antioch or as the number of these sees expanded into five in later centuries or as "primacy" became restricted to papal primacy or as the term was distinguished into a primacy of honor and/or jurisdiction. In this essay, "primacy" is used as a shorthand for papal primacy, while recognizing its very legitimate and ancient variations in meaning and in application.

One cannot escape this pervasive issue of language but only call attention to the systematic ambiguity of critical terms and then beg for those efforts of sympathetic understanding that make inquiry and mutual conversation possible.

---

10. Hermann J. Pottmeyer, *Unfehlbarkeit und Souveränität: Die päpstliche Unfehlbarkeit im System der ultramontanen Ekklesiologie des 19. Jahrhunderts*, Tübinger Theol. Studien 5 (Mainz: Grunewald, 1975).

The Method

The precision of the problem and the imprecision of the language introduce a consideration of method by which this question is to be pursued. Various strategies suggest themselves for this pattern of inquiry and discourse:

a. Standard manuals of theology cite any number of propositions touching upon the character of and the relationships obtaining between the primacy and the episcopate as in some way pertaining to faith. Theological notes such as *de fide divina definita, de fide definita, de fide catholica definita, de fide implicite definita* are salted liberally through the theses.[11] Should one attempt to execute the task assigned by combing through the "approved authors" (*auctores probati*) and sifting out those propositions or elements whose theological evaluation (*valor theologicus*) has been set so high and has received general agreement?

Serious reservations would attend such a settlement. Besides reducing this enterprise to a calculus of propositions, it would not meet the fundamental requirement set for this essay: that it should be *synthetic* (not summary) in character. The same unhappy results would obtain if one attempted a pastiche of papal or conciliar statements on the episcopate and the primacy. The historical occasions that made such a statement urgent in no way guarantee that it is either centrally or perennially important to the life and character of the Church or that either such a proposition or even congeries of such propositions would supply for the synthesis required. Synthesis — again, not summary — demands a principle of unity through which a diversity (here, of propositions) is drawn into coherence.

---

11. See, for example, Ioachim Salaverri, S.J., "De ecclesia Christi," in *Sacrae theologiae summa* (Madrid: BAC, 1955), tractate 3, vol. 1, 556, 569, 585, 597, 633, 656, etc.

b. Then again, one could comb not the manuals of theology nor the statements of the official magisterium, but the usages of history, ranging through the two thousand years of the Church, and by what John Stuart Mill called the "method of difference" separate off those elements whose presence was random or occasional or obviously historically conditioned and seize upon the remnant as those elements to be examined for "indispensability."[12] But this would create a history in which every later or isolated development was taken as accidental, a latter modification appended to an "essence" which had always been, with priority being given to origins as if these were comprehensively exhaustive. If lacunae are found within this history — for example, in the appeal to the Petrine texts during the early centuries of the Church — are these indications of what is "dispensable" as moments of an inadequate self-realization in the theology of the Church? As the historian James McCue has written: "There seems no reason to suppose *a priori* that the post-apostolic Church was immediately in such full possession of itself, of its own structure, that it immediately asserted (or assented to) the doctrine of the primacy of the bishop of Rome."[13] Just as the consciousness of the New Testament canon of scripture and the clear articulation of the doctrine on the episcopate and the apostolic succession, so have other doctrines come into their own over time — not the least being that of the primacy.

c. This essay will take the pattern for its argument from the charge that it be a synthetic consideration. The governing

---

12. John Stuart Mill, *A System of Logic,* 8th ed. (London: Longmans, Green, Reader, and Dyer, 1872), 452ff.

13. James F. McCue, "The Roman Primacy in the Second Century and the Problem of the Development of Doctrine," *Theological Studies* 25 (1964): 161; cited by Miller, *What Are They Saying about Papal Primacy?* 37.

concepts, furnishing the synthesis, will be those of relation and of unity or communion. The primacy and the episcopate are understood categorically as "relations," and these relations are given their character through their term, "communion." These two concepts have the possibility of unifying a great deal of the Church's teaching on the issue confronting this essay.

The actual doctrinal exploration of this essay will be preceded by two foundational considerations: chapter 1 deals with the subjective conditions for this inquiry and chapter 2 locates under the category of relation both primacy and episcopate. This metaphysical determination, in its turn, allows the specifically doctrinal considerations to begin with the issues of the foundation and of the term of the primacy and the episcopate in their service to the Church.

Ideology

Any attempt to explore this question engages the obvious difficulties attending so vast and historically complicated a subject matter. But these "obvious difficulties" may well not count as the greatest difficulties. Much more obfuscating can be the hidden drives and latent interests accruing not so much to the subject matter under consideration as to the conditions of subjectivity in which this consideration takes place. Stubbornly resistant to resolution may be not so much the problem under inquiry as the state of the one doing the inquiry. The dogmatic task bearing upon "essential and indispensable elements" would be naively miscast if it simply took for granted something that cannot be so easily assumed: the ordered intentionality of the one doing the consideration. One cannot presume the interior freedom that enables thinkers or dialogues or lines of inquiry to explore this general subject matter with honesty, objectivity, and the necessary detachment. Why not? Because in so many different ways, one is dealing with power (*potestas*).[14]

The history of the discussions of power, importance, and eminence, of being "first," of honor and jurisdiction — both within as well as outside the Church — centuries of councils and conferences, inquiries, arrogant claims and actions, intractable debates and final alienations that emerged precisely from this present subject matter, indicate how profoundly difficult it is to treat questions of power in any other than a defensive, aggressive, minatory, or self-serving way. Not impossible, but very difficult! Everything that Jürgen Habermas has written about the distortions occasioned by "interest" finds its embodiment in human history and in the history of theology.[15] Driven by unfaced "interest," the protagonists, while seeming to do theology, can actually be framing ideologies — theoretical justifications for either the current allocations of power or for radical changes demanded in the possession and uses of power. One can only smile, for example, when theories are elaborated to justify papal primacy in the granting of jurisdiction by contending that Peter assigned territories to the individual apostles.[16] On the other hand, a similar reaction can be elicited by article 4 of the *Smalcald Articles* that "the papacy is of no use to the Church because

---

14. It is remarkable to note there is rather a dearth in Catholic theology on the subject of power, Karl Rahner's essay "A Theology of Power" constituting an exception; see *Theological Investigations* 4, trans. Kevin Smyth (Baltimore: Helicon Press, 1966), 391–409.

15. Jürgen Habermas, "Knowledge and Interest," in *Sociological Theory and Philosophical Analysis*, ed. Dorothy Emmet and Alasdair MacIntyre (New York: Macmillan, 1970), 36–54; Henning Ottmann, "Cognitive Interests and Self-Reflection," in *Habermas: Critical Debates*, ed. John B. Thompson and David Held (Cambridge: MIT Press, 1982), 79–97.

16. Henn, "Historical-Theological Synthesis," 228 n. 38.

it exercises no Christian office."[17] John B. Thompson has put it accurately: "To study ideology...is to study the ways in which meaning (or signification) serves to sustain relations of domination."[18]

This is not to suggest that ideology is conscious deception. It can obtain with great good will and blindness about one's actual motivation. It is classically true that the "will-to-power" often operates at so unconscious a level that its real motivational drive is hidden from the very ones framing the theories that embody it. At its lightest, such "theology" is transparent in its tactics; at its worst, it does not emerge from faith, but from bad faith and the unfaced drives of self-interest.[19]

The will-to-power constitutes one of the strongest, yet

---

17. As cited in Fred Kramer, "A Lutheran Understanding of Papal Primacy," in *Papal Primacy and the Universal Church,* ed. Paul Empie and T. Austin Murphy (Minneapolis: Augsburg, 1974), 130.

18. As cited by Terry Eagleton, *Ideology: An Introduction* (London: Verso, 1991), 5. Eagleton comments that this is probably the single most widely accepted understanding of ideology today. Obviously, the term is multivalent, possessing variant meanings throughout the history of thought. For another contemporary use, more positive than the one used in this essay, see George F. Kennan, *Around the Cragged Hill* (New York: W. W. Norton, 1993), 96–107.

19. Eagleton suggests that there are at least six different strategies in the process of legitimation of an ideology, none of which has been stranger to the history of Catholic theology: "A dominant power may legitimate itself by *promoting* beliefs and value congenial to it; *naturalizing* and *universalizing* such beliefs so as to render them self-evident and apparently inevitable; *denigrating* ideas which might challenge it; *excluding* rival forms of thought, perhaps by some unspoken but systematic logic; and *obscuring* social reality in ways convenient to itself. Such 'mystification,' as it is commonly known, frequently takes the form of masking or suppressing social conflicts, from which arises the conception of ideology as an imaginary resolution of real contradiction. In any actual ideological formation, all six of these strategies are likely to interact in complex ways" (5–6). For the thematic history of this term from Destutt de Tracy through Marxism, see David Hawkes, *Ideology* (New York: Routledge, 1996).

unrecognized passions within human engagements, and the history of the Church indicates how ravaging and destructive an effect it can produce even while advancing under the flag of the most religious of vocabularies. William Henn has summarized something of its influence: "It is difficult to read the various pretentious claims to power which mark the history of the relation between primacy and episcopacy during the second millennium without feeling a certain lack of ease before the gospel passages in which Jesus corrects the apostles for wanting to be the greatest."[20] So much in the past centuries must persuade one that unless ideology is faced and checked, there is no possibility of an ecumenically successful theology of leadership, governance, teaching, and direction. Such a theology requires something along the line of the *praeambula purificationis* that serves as chapter 1 of this essay.

---

20. Henn, "Historical-Theological Synthesis," 262.

CHAPTER ONE

The Conditions for the Inquiry: Towards Purity of Heart

From its origins, Christian spirituality has recognized that passion, desires, and disordered attachment to any form of power inevitably distort reflection. For this reason, this tradition has been classically concerned with the prior need for purity of heart, the undeviating determination of will and affectivity upon God. Purity of heart was the primordial concern of Cassian in the *Conferences of the Abbot Moses;* in the Ignatian *Spiritual Exercises* it becomes the conquest of disordered affectivity in order to search and find the divine will in the disposition of one's life; and it forms the goal of the Night of the Senses in John of the Cross.

One might turn to any of these spiritual masters for that graced maturation of human transcendentality that allows for a theology — rather than an ideology — of the primacy or the episcopate, but it is John of the Cross whom I should like to adopt for our purposes. In chapter 13 of the First Book of the *Ascent of Mount Carmel*, John offers three counsels — *el modo breve* — for the development of this purity of heart, three counsels that "if they are faithfully put into practice, are quite sufficient for entrance into the night of the senses."[1] Something like these three seem essential if theologians or bishops or general discussions are to move beyond

---

1. Juan de la Cruz, *Subida del Monte Carmelo* I.13, no. 8, in *Vida y obras de San Juan de la Cruz,* ed. Crisógono de Jesús, Matías del Niño

disordered affectivity in serious consideration of the usages of power. Perhaps Catholic theologians who hope that their explorations of directive authority remain faithful to the patterns and spirit of Christ can adapt them to this project. They may ring a bit stark, but they ring no less so in John of the Cross himself.

First, the governing desire of those investigating and weighing this issue must be, for themselves as for the constitution of the Church itself, "to imitate Christ in everything they do, conforming themselves to His life."[2] Everything else in theological assertions and decisions must take its direction from this primordial focus upon Jesus as method, as way. That means concretely that meditation and the study of His life must contextualize theological reflection upon the uses of power and position. Only this steady presence and challenge of the life of Jesus can enable one to understand how this life can be imitated in the structures of authority and mission within the Church.

Second, in order that this theological reflection might proceed soundly, every suggestion of power and prestige, of honor and directive preeminence, of jurisdiction, domination, and divine right that presents itself in theory or in practice or in symbol — either to obtain or to continue — if it is not actually seen and understood "purely" (*puramente*) as necessary to further the glory of God, must be renounced for that love and imitation of Christ sketched by the first counsel. This renunciation is demanded of those who are in positions of power, of those who aspire to some form of power, and of those whose bitter experience issues out

---

Jesús, and Lucinio del SS. Sacramento (Madrid: BAC, 1964), 391; ET: *The Complete Works of John of the Cross,* trans. and ed. Kieran Kavanaugh and Otilio Rodriguez (Washington, D.C.: ICS, 1991).

2. Juan de la Cruz, *Subida* I.13, nos. 1 and 3, 390; *Complete Works,* 147–48.

of a desire for power denied. For in all cases, whether in defense, in aspiration, or in resentment, what may well be operative — as powerfully as it is latent — is a disordered will-to-power.

In this counsel, the imitation of Christ becomes concretely embodied in the motive that governed His life, a motive that can be phrased many different ways: the glory of God, the accomplishment of God's will (John 4:34). In *Ut unum sint,* the pope forcibly makes the same appeal, the same condition, as he fosters those inquiries into "a way of exercising the primacy which, while in no way renouncing what is essential to its [papal] mission, is nonetheless open to a new situation."[3] What should govern and drive this inquiry? The papal answer is: "keeping in mind only the will of Christ for his Church" ("in mente habentes tantummodo Christi voluntatem erga suam Ecclesiam").[4] Only if the theological discussion searches into Christ's will for His Church does the project initiated by the pope have any chance of moving beyond ideology to theology.

Third, to discover what is actually for the glory of God, it is necessary to counter positively an innately regressive but disguised will-to-power that can underlie, influence, and even govern human judgment in a thousand hidden ways. Thus it is necessary "to strive to be inclined" ("procure siempre inclinarse") not to what is more powerful, but what is less powerful; not to what is more dominant, but what is less dominant; not for positions of extensive control, but for what is genuine and hidden service; not for what is most prestigious and preeminent, but what is least.

This does not mean that one will not finally frame or jus-

---

3. *Ut unum sint,* no. 95, in *AAS* 95:11 (November 10, 1995): 977–78; ET: *Origins* 25, no. 4 (June 8, 1995): 69 (m).

4. *Ut unum sint,* no. 96, in *AAS,* 978; *Origins,* 70 (m).

tify a position of even extensive power and jurisdiction as doctrine demanded by the mandate of Christ. But one has a much greater chance of coming to these positions or structures as an authentic realization of "the will of Christ for His Church" if one is habitually and antecedently suspicious of accruing power, preeminence, and honor. Such a detachment or interior freedom makes it more possible to discover what is true. Thus an ascetical "hermeneutics of suspicion" can ground a strategy to check the natural drive for preeminence and power. It can aid one to move beyond these enormously powerful, regressive appetites and their resultant self-deceptions in order to find the divine will in the disposition of the Church's constitution.

The deep asceticism and contemplative spirit that make for purity of heart together with its contextualizing, empowering, and requisite hermeneutics of suspicion do not resolve these issues for the theologian, but they are the indispensable conditions for the possibility of any authentic resolution. For one cannot simply take for granted that one possesses such an undeviating determination towards the will of God that *Ut unum sint* encourages theologians and bishops to seek.[5] Yet without this radical purification of sub-

---

5. The divisions within the Church consequent upon the disordered desire for power provoked this comment from Joseph Ratzinger: "Does this not recall in terrible fashion that quarrelling began even among Christ's disciples for the places to the right and to the left of the master, that is, for the offices in the coming messianic kingdom? And ought it not to recall to both sides the words of the Lord, that the greatest must be as the least, and the servant of all. This is not to do away with the office; the mandate to Peter and the mandate to the apostles are not withdrawn. But it is a demand of ultimate urgency addressed both to those who, vested with the office, are preachers of the word, and to their listeners. To the former, that they should strive to be in very truth *servi servorum Dei;* to the latter, not to refuse to be outwardly the 'last' in order to know, in humble joy, that, precisely thus and not otherwise, they are first. Only if both — those in office and those without — seek the spirit of the Gospel in un-

jectivity, the transcendental conditions for the treatment of the issues inherent within this task are not present. Only purity of heart will enable a discussion that is not governed by ambition or fear or a desire to curry favor or by Oedipal resentments and the frustrated consciousness of powerlessness. Only purity of heart will make it possible to come to and speak the truth about the primacy and the episcopate.

---

conditional integrity can there be hope for a union of those who would never have been torn asunder without a denial of this spirit" (Joseph Ratzinger, "Primacy, Episcopate, and Apostolic Succession," in Karl Rahner and Joseph Ratzinger, *The Episcopate and the Primacy* [New York: Herder and Herder, 1963], 63).

CHAPTER TWO

Metaphysical Parameters: Primacy and Episcopate as Relations

This brings this inquiry to its initial and fundamental question: when one talks about the primacy and the episcopate, what kind of thing is under discussion? Where does one locate these words in their most generic meaning? To phrase this same question another way: what is the fundamental category for our understanding of "the primacy" and "the episcopate"?

This is not an idle question. Gilbert Ryle has sharply drawn the attention of contemporary analytic philosophy to the damage done to inquiry by "category mistakes," i.e., "the presentation of facts belonging to one category in the idioms appropriate to another" — what Armand Maurer has stylized "the mistake of trying to make one category do the work of another."[1] Ignore the radical pluralism of things, what Aristotle called "the categories of being," and one treats all reality as if it were simply the same kind of thing. This confusion of semantic categories gives rise to

---

1. Gilbert Ryle, "Categories," *Logic and Language,* ed. Antony Flew, second series (Brookfield, Vt.: Basil Blackwell, 1993), 65–81, cited in Armand A. Maurer, "English Philosophy," in Etienne Gilson, Thomas Langan, and Armand A. Maurer, *Recent Philosophy: Hegel to the Present* (New York: Random House, 1966), 546–47.

nonsensical assertions and inconclusive arguments. This has been noted as peculiarly true in the misrepresentation of social reality by "reification."[2]

There are, for example, human beings and there is the state. Both are, in their own sense, real. But they are not the same kind of thing. They are not "real" in the same way. If the state is simply taken as a bigger kind of human being, one has Thomas Hobbes and the Leviathan. Again, it is not without forensic value to hypostasize a multinational corporation as a "moral person." But fail to bear in mind that this is a metaphor for legal purposes, and one gives such complex entities a dignity and a primary importance that is radically distorted.

Hypostatic language has made valuable contributions to the exploration of the Church, but this becomes dangerously misleading if the image is taken for the letter. The bull *Unam sanctam* could seem to make continuous use of "body" as if it were a literal predicate of the Church. It argued to the unity of Christ and pope because "there is one body of the one and unique Church, one head, not two heads as if it were a monster, i.e., Christ and Peter, the vicar of Christ, and the successor of Peter."[3] Even a theologian as significant as the great Karl Rahner argued in a similar manner to the priority of the college of bishops: "As a juridical personal-

---

2. See Joseph A. Komonchak, "The Epistemology of Reception," *The Jurist* 57 (1997).

3. "Ecclesiae unius et unicae unum corpus, unum caput, non duo capita quasi monstrum, Christus videlicet et Christi vicarius Petrus, Petrique successor" (*Unam sanctam* [DS 872]). Klaus Schatz also notes the argument of *Unam sanctam*, "starting from a seamless understanding of the Church as unit and leading the *reductio ad unum* to its ultimate consequence, that the one Church could not be like a deformed child with two heads" (Klaus Schatz, *Papal Primacy: From Its Origins to the Present,* trans. John A. Otto and Linda M. Maloney [Collegeville, Minn.: Liturgical Press, 1996], 85).

ity, sacramentally based and hence sustained by the Spirit of
God, this inclusive unity precedes (objectively) the individual bishop as such."[4] But "juridical personality" is a legal
fiction. The question must be asked: what is ontologically
predicated of the college of bishops that allows this college
to be a recipient of this priority? Hence, in this essay also, it
is critical to determine what kind of primordial, ontological
significance or kind of thing is engaged when talking about
"the episcopate" and "the primacy." It should be stressed
that this precision in ontology is not to rule out corporate,
organic metaphors whose contributions to theology have
been immense, but to distinguish "language games" — to use
Wittgenstein's classic phrase — in which they are appropriate
from those in which they are not.

This categorical probing indicates immediately that what
is at issue in the discussion of primacy and the episcopate are
not autonomous things or objects nor their self-referential or
intrinsic modifications — in scholastic parlance, that is, primacy and episcopate are neither substances directly or the
qualities inherent in substances. "Primacy" and "episcopate"
are each an abstraction: "primacy," for the leadership of the
bishop of Rome, the primate; "episcopate," for the collectivity of bishops, for the episcopate, precisely as episcopate, i.e.,
in their relationship to one another and collectively to the
Church as a whole. (Perhaps, one might argue, the terms of
the topic assigned should have been kept on the same level,
i.e., "primacy and episcopacy" or "the primate and the episcopate"; the advantage of the present formulation, however,
is that it does not terminologically separate the primate from
the episcopate.)

---

4. Karl Rahner, "The Hierarchical Structure of the Church with Special Reference to the Episcopate" (commentary on chapter 3 of *Lumen
gentium*), in *Commentary on the Documents of Vatican II*, ed. Herbert
Vorgrimler (New York: Crossroad, 1989), 1:198.

If one selects from the Aristotelian schema of the radical pluralism in beings and in terms, then "primacy" and "episcopate" must be categorized as relations — either directly or obliquely, as the words denote either the relationship itself ("primacy") or the bearers/subjects of a set of relationships under the formality of that relationship ("episcopate"). "Relation" is the category primordially predicated of each of these realities; and everything about them, if it is to be asserted ontologically, must attend to their radically relational character. For "episcopate" and "primacy" do not indicate simply things in themselves, but only subjects as denominated in or by means of their relationship to others. These theological relationships engage the persons, the individual units or the referents of language, in which they exist not in some autonomous self-sufficiency or distinction, but only in their reference to something else — to an other (πρός τι). As Aquinas put it: "Relation differs from quantity and quality in this: because quantity and quality are accidents remaining in a subject; relation, however, as Boethius says, signifies something not as remaining in the subject, but as passing from it to something else."[5] Primacy and episcopate are ways of being *ad aliud.*

"Primacy" obviously is this: something is "first" only in relationship to those that are "not first." Further, if primacy is dynamic — i.e., if primacy is to effect something in something else — then it obtains its character from the effect it works on those who are not first, who are "second" because they

---

5. "Relatio in hoc differt a quantitate et qualitate: quia quantitas et qualitas sunt quaedam accidentia in subiecto remanentia; relatio autem non significat, ut Boëtius dicit, ut in subiecto manes, sed ut in transitu quodam ad aliud" (St. Thomas Aquinas, *Quaestiones disputatae de potentia Dei*, ed. Paul Pession [Turin: Marietti, 1949], VII. 8; ET: Thomas Aquinas, *On the Power of God* [London: Burns, Oates & Washbourne, 1934], III. 47 [m]).

receive an influence from another. It is in virtue of this effect that it is called "the primacy." Another way of making the same assertion: since the primacy is called in *Pastor aeternus* a principle or source of the unity of the episcopate and of the faithful, then in this it must be and can only be understood relationally, that is, by that of which it is the principle.

"Episcopate" denotes a twofold relationship: the one that denominates the bishops by means of one another in some solidarity — later to be spelled out as college; the other that indicates their Christian leadership in reference to all the members of the Christian community. The generic intelligibility of "episcopate" lies in a position of sacramental ministry and jurisdictional authority shared in relationship among the bishops and exercised in relationship to still other Catholics. This complicated dual relationship inherent in "episcopate" may underlie something of the problem whether the primary relationship of a bishop is to his fellow bishops in college or to the members of his diocese.

To understand how both primacy and episcopate must be conceived and analyzed as relations, one must see both as order or orientation: "There must be order in things themselves, and this order is a kind of relation," wrote Aquinas.

> Wherefore there must be relations in things themselves, whereby one is ordered to another. Now one thing is ordered to another either by reason of quantity or by reason of active and passive power [*secundum virtutem activam seu passivam*]: for on these two counts alone is something observed in one that has reference to an external other. For a thing is measured not only by its intrinsic quantity, but also in reference to an extrinsic quantity. And again by its active power, one thing acts on another, and by its passive power, one thing is acted upon by another.[6]

---

6. Aquinas, *De potentia Dei* VII. 9. ET: III. 53 (m).

It is precisely through the conferral of active and passive powers and their exercise that the Church places certain human beings in a profound orientation to others, a relationship of service whose activities are spelled out in the triple *munera* of teaching, sanctifying, and governing.

This predicamental identification of episcopate and primacy as relations rules out the literal idiom of organic development or substantial growth in any proper sense. One must, of course, recognize that substantial vocabulary — such as "body" and "organism" or "juridical personality" — as helpful and illuminatingly metaphorical, even indispensable. But to take it as literal, ontological predication is to make a "category mistake." A predicamental relation is not a substantial thing. A woman is not essentially designated by "mother," nor is a man by "worker." As the Thomistic metaphysics of relations has figured importantly in trinitarian theology and in social theory, developing significantly the Aristotelian understanding, perhaps it can contribute helpfully to the grasp of primacy and episcopate as well.

"A relation that is found in things [i.e., a real relation]," wrote Aquinas, "consists in the order of one thing to another."[7] It is crucial to note that it is the term — that towards which the subject by and in this *ordo* is oriented — that gives character or intelligibility or definition (*ratio*) to the relationship. As a parent is denoted by the reality of the child or the worker by his industrial product, so the character of any relation is determined and disclosed by that to which the subject is referred. As Aristotle put it: "If a relative is definitely known, that to which it is relative will

---

7. "Relatio, quae est in rebus, consistit in ordine quodam unius rei ad aliam" (St. Thomas Aquinas, *In duodecim libros metaphysicorum Aristotelis expositio* [Turin: Marietti, 1950], V. 17, no. 1004).

then be as definitely known. What is more, we may call this self-evident."[8]

This dependence of the character or intelligibility of the relation upon the term of the relationship must be seen as bearing importantly upon primacy and episcopacy. As Aquinas wrote, in agreement with Aristotle: "The character [*ratio*] of a relation — as one finds also in the case of motion — depends upon the end or the term, just as its existence [*esse*] depends upon the subject."[9] The character (*ratio*) of a relation he distinguishes from its existence (*esse*). The character of a relation depends upon the term; the existence of a relation depends upon the subject that possesses the relation. As predicamental realities, the existence of primacy and episcopacy is *esse in* — they are real qualifications of their subjects, i.e., of pope and bishops; as relations, their character and total intelligibility (*ratio*) is *ad aliud* — they get their meaning or intelligibility from that towards which the relation points.

This may seem unduly abstract, but its pertinence should become evident. Perhaps a single proleptic example: If "primacy" embodies "an order of one thing to another" — of pope to the unity of the bishops, for example — and if the very character of that relationship of primacy depends upon that to which it is ordered, then it is not enough to

---

8. Aristotle, *Categories*, VII. 8a37–40. Aristotle indicates how self-evident this is by example: "For suppose that you definitely know a particular thing to be 'double'; then at once will you definitely know also that thing of which it is double. You cannot know that it is double without knowing that it is double of something specific and definite" (8b4–8); Greek and English text in Aristotle, *The Categories, On Interpretation*, ed. and trans. Harold P. Cook, Loeb Classical Library (Cambridge, Mass.: Harvard University Press, 1962), 60–61.

9. "Ratio relationis, sicut et motus, dependet ex fine vel termino, sicut esse eius dependet ex subiecto" (Thomas Aquinas, *Summa theologiae*, III. 2. 7. ad 2).

say that the First Vatican Council dealt with the primacy and did not get around to episcopate. One cannot understand the primacy adequately without understanding what is the real character of the unity of the episcopate. Or, more positively, as the Church progressively understands the episcopate more adequately, its understanding of the primacy will likewise and correlatively develop. The episcopate specifies the intelligibility of the primacy.

Granted that "episcopate" and "primacy" denote relationships, one further factor must be brought to mind. At stake here is not simply a relation of one "thing" to another, but a relation of persons: primacy relates one person to many; episcopate relates persons in community to others. What Martin Buber, cited by Emmanuel Lévinas, wrote of the human person is profoundly operative in the ontology of primacy and episcopate: "The human person can become whole not by virtue of a relation to himself, but only by virtue of a relation to another self."[10] The whole meaning of the primacy and the episcopate is found in their others, their correlative terms. The others as the personal terms of the relationships of the primacy and the episcopate will determine their character and indicate their present health.

This predicamental identification of episcopate and primacy within the category of relation makes it possible to ask with greater precision what is indispensable. As has been stated, every predicamental real relation is bifurcated: it possesses its existence (*esse*) in its subject as a real or ontological inherent in its subject; it possesses its character or intelligibility (*ratio*) through its term. What is indispensable for a relation is what is necessary for its foundation and its term,

---

10. Emmanuel Lévinas, "Martin Buber and the Theory of Knowledge," *The Lévinas Reader* (Oxford: Blackwell, 1994), 66 (m).

i.e., what brings it into being and sustains it in existence (*esse*) and what gives it its character (*ratio*).

The question of this essay, then, becomes twofold: (1) what is the activity that stands as foundational to primacy and episcopacy, i.e., what activity brings them into being and what activity sustains them precisely as this kind of relationship? (2) what are the terms of each of these relations, what is each relative to and what, consequently, gives them their character? The first of these two questions can be taken here, leaving to subsequent chapters the fuller and more elaborate treatment of the second question, as it is that question that constitutes the issue for this essay.

1. If the primacy and the episcopate are both complicated relations, what lies as their basis? Here we must distinguish what brings them into being and what sustains them continually as relations. Here one may call on the determinations of Vatican II.

First, they are brought into being by the communication of God's own Spirit by Christ, a communication sacramentally actualized and specified in episcopal ordination — what the *Nota explicativa praevia* spoke of as *consecratio* — and its resultant "ontological participation in the sacred functions (ontologica participatio sacrorum munerum)," that is, orders; secondly, canonical or juridical determination (canonica seu iuridica determinatio) places the bishop within the concrete relationships in and through which these *munera* are to be exercised in hierarchical communion with the head of the college and its members, that is, jurisdiction; thirdly, the triple *munera* (teaching, sanctifying, and governing) — both as lasting, active *potentiae* (office) and as activities in which these *potentiae* are realized (functions) — permanently serve as the foundation for the relation of the bishops to one another (collegiality and primacy) and to the people of God. Each of these three requires a more precise explanation.

The sacrament of episcopal consecration confers the triple *munera*, by which the relationship of an individual bishop to the other bishops is generally secured and his relationship to the Church generally stated. But in order that the *munus regendi*, the office of governing — as well as the other two *munera* — can come into actual exercise, can emerge from within, it is obviously necessary that there be someone to govern, to teach, and to sanctify. There must be a concrete determination of the subjects that bear the term of the relationship. This canonical determination does not endow one with the triple *munera*, but it does designate a specific office or a special community, a local church, in which he is to exercise the triple *munera*, by which he is related to others.

So *Lumen gentium* taught that the foundation both for primacy — as an episcopal reality — and for the episcopate in general is sacramental, while hierarchical communion "situates the exercise of the sacramentally based offices of the bishop within the context of a college, comprised of head and members."[11] To cite *Lumen gentium:* "A person is constituted a member of the episcopal body by virtue of sacramental consecration and by hierarchical communion with the head and members of the college."[12] Consecration confers the triple *munera;* but just as fire cannot heat unless there is something to be heated nor can a teacher teach unless there is someone to be taught, so the triple *munera* cannot be exercised unless there is a concrete determination on how they are to be exercised and in regard

---

11. William Henn, O.F.M. Cap., "Historical-Theological Synthesis of the Relation between Primacy and Episcopacy during the Second Millennium," *Il primato del successore de Pietro: Atti del simposio teologico, Roma, dicembre 1996* (Vatican City: Libreria Editrice Vaticana, 1997), 255.

12. "Membrum corporis episcopalis aliquis constituitur vi sacramentalis consecrationis et hierarchica communione cum collegii capite atque membris" (*Lumen gentium,* chap. 3, no. 22; Tanner, *Decrees,* 2:866).

to whom. Orders — episcopal consecration — confer the threefold *munera,* of teaching, sanctifying, and governing; canonical determination supplies the conditions necessary for the exercise of the three *munera.* The sacramental action serves as the foundation for the coming-to-be of that relation that is episcopacy and primacy, while the determination to a particular Church or for a particular office within hierarchical communion is the further specification of the foundation for primacy and the relation of a bishop to his diocese. The actual abiding foundation is the triple *munera* within hierarchical communion.

The triple *munera* exist both as habitual potencies and as the actual exercises of these potentialities. In and through both, the episcopate is ordered within itself and towards the faithful. While episcopal ordination is the foundation for the coming-to-be of the episcopate, the active and passive *potentiae* and the consequent activities of the triple *munera* in hierarchical communion are the abiding foundation for the relationship that is episcopacy.[13] The active and passive potencies of the triple *munera* are to be realized in their activities, and these have others for their term. Hence, they found the relations that are primacy and episcopacy. "Relative beings of this kind are relative in two ways: in one way, according to active and passive potency; and in a second way, according to the actualization of these potencies, which are to act and to undergo."[14] The triple *munera,* either as active potencies or as actualized activities, serve as the imme-

---

13. *Lumen gentium,* "Nota explicativa praevia," no. 2; Tanner, *Decrees,* 2:899.

14. "Huiusmodi relativa sunt relative dupliciter. Uno modo, secundum *potentiam* activam et passivam; et secundo modo, secundum *actus* harum potentiarum, qui sunt agere et pati" (Thomas Aquinas, *In meta.* V. 17. no. 1023; ET: St. Thomas Aquinas, *Commentary on the Metaphysics of Aristotle,* trans. John P. Rowan [Chicago: Henry Regnery, 1961], 1:387 [m]; emphasis added).

diate foundations in virtue of which primacy and episcopacy
are formally ordered *ad aliud*. The permanent participation
in the triple *munera* remains forever a received sacramental
modification of the subject, orienting the pope or the bishop
or the episcopate to others.

But "Church" introduces the more radical foundation of
all of these potencies and activities — sacramental and jurisdictional. It is the Church that serves as the more basic
ground for primacy and episcopacy, the community that is
the people of God. It is essential that *Lumen gentium* in elab-
orating an understanding of the Church and its offices spoke
first of the mystery of the Church and then of the people of
God. In these two first chapters, the Dogmatic Constitution
on the Church set out the context, conditions, and community in which all special ministries exist, and thus laid the
foundation for an understanding of office and official ministries in the Church — as the foundation is the principle out
of which issues the relationship. That means that the mystery of the Church and the people of God constitute the real
source for office and, hence, for the primacy and the episcopate. Only understood as emerging from this foundation is
either relationship intelligible.[15]

2. One way in which an orientation or relational order
can obtain is "as one thing receives something from another or gives something to another."[16] The relational term
of episcopate and primacy — the personal term — gives the
character to each relation. They are constituted and defined
by the correlative terms to which their appropriate activities,
the triple *munera*, are ordered. As a result of this sacramental and jurisdictional activity, the bishops of the Church and

---

15. I am grateful to Peter Hünermann for discussions on this subject.
16. Thomas Aquinas, *In meta. libro,* V. Lectio 17, no. 1004.

the bishop of Rome stand in a particular relationship to one another and to the Church as a whole.

The question naturally emerges: if both primacy and episcopate denote relationships, founded on and realized in activities and passivities, and if they are dynamically oriented towards particular functions, then they — like any such relation — receive their fundamental character from that towards which they are oriented: "from what they give to something else." The question becomes: what do the primacy and the episcopate give to something else? More concretely, how do they serve the Church? In examining the episcopate and the primacy, then, to determine what is indispensable and what is not, the inquiry falls heavily upon what are the *terms* of these relationships and what are the *functions* appropriate to them. This brings us to the issue proper to this essay: what is the relationship between the primacy and the episcopate?

One must insist that, like the Church itself, the primacy and episcopate exist only in the concrete circumstances of history. This has been the burden of recent historical studies and particularly of those that preceded and informed this essay. They are presupposed here.

CHAPTER THREE

Primacy and Its Ministry
to a Twofold Unity

The primacy is a relationship — classically of jurisdiction — according to which a certain purpose and function become definitionally critical.[1] The subject of this relationship is the bishop of Rome, established in this relationship by episcopal consecration and the canonical determination that specifies his exercise of the triple *munera* (*esse*); but the intelligibility or character (*ratio*) of the relationship lies with its term. What is this term that discloses the nature, the primacy of the bishop of Rome? What is primacy "for"?

The normative treatment of this question in the modern Church can be found in the opening paragraphs of *Pastor aeternus,* and, indeed, it is important to consider the entire Dogmatic Constitution on the Church from Vatican I through these initial paragraphs. They are critical not only to determine what is principally at stake in this constitution, but also to understand why it is that the Dogmatic Constitution on the Church of the Second Vatican Council is actually a legitimate development and not a repudiation of the fundamental directions set by this earlier council. The way *Pastor aeternus* has been distorted in its reading has influenced ecclesiology for almost one hundred years.

---

1. *Pastor aeternus*, chap. 3 (DS 3064); Tanner, *Decrees*, 2:814.

To be more concrete: it is curious that discussions of the Petrine ministry in the contemporary Church have become focused upon the issue of papal infallibility. The discussions of this prerogative have become so disproportionate to its actual use that they have obscured the usual, day-by-day papal magisterium and gathered to themselves the principal attention regarding the primacy.

But Garret Sweeney, following Edmond Dublanchy, has calculated that papal dogmatic definitions are really quite rare: some twelve over two thousand years. Such a definition, judges Sweeney, occurred first in the Tome of Leo and no more than four more times until the Reformation and *Exsurge Domine;* the seventeenth century saw another four within sixty years leveled against Jansenism and Quietism; finally there were the condemnation of the Synod of Pistoia in 1794 and the two Marian definitions of the past centuries.[2] But even this modest enumeration seems excessive. Klaus Schatz reduces this list to seven and Francis A. Sullivan agrees with this reduction.[3] Excepting the last two definitions, Sweeney comments:

---

2. Garrett Sweeney, "The Forgotten Council," in *Bishops and Writers: Aspects of the Evolution of Modern English Catholicism,* ed. Adrian Hastings (Wheathampstead: Anthony Clarke, 1977), 173–74. Sweeney makes this pertinent observation: "History bears out the teaching of Vatican I, that such [papal definitions] are the last desperate resort of the faithful when all other means of authentification have failed." The first of such papal definitions was the Tome of Leo: "It was the age of Attila and of Genseric and communications were already breaking down." For Edmond Dublanchy, see *Dictionnaire de théologie catholique,* 7:1703–4. Louis Billot is in agreement with Dublanchy's list. See his *Tractatus de Ecclesia Christi,* 1st ed. (Rome: Gregoriana, 1898), 657–59 (2d ed., 1903, 658–60). See Francis A. Sullivan, S.J., *Creative Fidelity: Weighing and Interpreting Documents of the Magisterium* (New York: Paulist, 1995), 84–85, 193 n. 14.

3. See Sullivan, *Creative Fidelity,* 84–92.

Each of these occasions was in some way an example of a "special condition," which, to revert to the words of Gasser at the [First Vatican] Council, called for the exercise of a "special privilege." But special conditions do not recur as regularly as the changing seasons. They belong to particular moments in the history of the Church and such moments may never occur again.[4]

Whatever one judges to be the frequency or future of papal definitions whose irreformability is "of themselves, and not by the consent of the Church" ("ex sese, non autem ex consensu Ecclesiae"),[5] *Pastor aeternus* takes as its explicit purpose not the determination of these very rare or occasional moments when the Roman Pontiff participates in that infallibility that Christ willed His Church to possess, but the more extensive and pervasive relation of the primacy of which irreformable definitions are only one and an exceptional instantiation. Pius IX, "with the approval of the sacred council" ("sacro approbante concilio"), proposed to set forth "doctrine concerning the institution, permanence, and nature of the sacred and apostolic primacy" ("doctrinam de institutione, perpetuitate ac natura sacri apostolici primatus").[6] Far more crucial to the life of the Church is not the issue of papal definitions, but the issue and nature of papal primacy.

Even in teaching, the major issue is not papal infallibility but the supreme magisterial authority as an aspect of the primacy.[7] A discussion of the primacy must include the primatial magisterium, which is not simply to be identified with infallibility. It is a question of the special role of the primate in definitive decisions on matters of faith, whether with a

---

4. Sweeney, "The Forgotten Council," 174.

5. *Pastor aeternus,* chap. 4 (DS 3074); Tanner, *Decrees,* 2:816 (m).

6. *Pastor aeternus,* Prologus (DS 3052); Tanner, *Decrees,* 2:811–12.

7. *Pastor aeternus,* chap. 4 (DS 3065); Tanner, *Decrees,* 2:815.

council or apart from one.[8] It must be also noted that when
Pastor aeternus introduces this declaration on the primacy of
the bishop of Rome, it does so not in terms of a tradition of
power, but in terms of purpose or the *munus* of the primacy.
The *munus* spells out the purpose of the primacy.

"To render permanent the saving work of redemption,"
Christ determined to build a Church in which all of the faithful would be united with one another "by/in the bond of
one faith and charity."[9] This paired unity required that there
should be first apostles, then shepherds and teachers until the
consummation of the ages. But in order that

> (1) the episcopate [*episcopatus*] itself should be one and un-
> divided, and that, (2) by means of a close union among the
> priests [*per cohaerentes sibi invicem sacerdotes*], the whole
> multitude of believers should be held together in the unity
> of faith and communion [*in fidei et communionis unitate*],
> Christ set blessed Peter over the rest of the apostles and insti-
> tuted in him a permanent principle (source) of both unities
> and their visible foundation [*perpetuum utriusque unitatis
> principium ac visible fundamentum*].[10]

Pastor aeternus is asserting as foundational to its entire argument that the purpose of the Petrine ministry — whether
exercised by Peter in the primitive Christian community or
by his successors in the subsequent history of the Church —
focused directly upon unity. And this unity is twofold, the
parts of which are dynamically related: the primacy was to
foster initially (1) unity within the episcopate, the unity of
the bishops among themselves, (2) and then, by means of
(*per*) that unity, the unity of the members of the Church.
The unity of the episcopate was the condition and the agency

---

8. Francis A. Sullivan, S.J., *Magisterium* (New York: Paulist, 1983),
62–78.

9. *Pastor aeternus,* Prologus (DS 3050); Tanner, *Decrees,* 2:811.

10. *Pastor aeternus,* Prologus (DS 3051); Tanner, *Decrees,* 2:811–12
(m); enumeration added.

through which the unity of the Church would be realized —
a unity specified as that in faith and communion, to which
the contradictory would be heresy and schism. "The unity in
faith and communion": this phrase could be used as a par-
allel for the previous "bond of one faith and charity," and
"communion" would develop importantly and crucially in
the ecclesiology of the next hundred years.

Thus *Pastor aeternus* taught that there are two terms of
the relationship that is the primacy. First, in his primacy,
the pope relates to the episcopate to foster its unity — specified in the document for all as a unity in authentic faith and
effective/affective charity or communion. Secondly, in his primacy and in and with and through the episcopate, the pope
relates to all the faithful by fostering their unity in authentic faith and communion. The episcopate is not simply an
instrument of papal primacy, but constitutes a unity with
the primacy (as will be seen) that fosters unity in the faithful. The constitution calls the primacy, then, "a permanent
principle [source] of both unities and their visible foundation."[11] As a principle or source, the primacy is relationally
defined by that of which it is the principle — and that is a
twofold unity: the unity of the episcopate and the unity of
the faithful.

This care for a twofold unity has habitually defined the
purpose of the primacy and is obviously definitionally indispensable, for the term of the relationship is also its
purpose. *Pastor aeternus* understands the primacy as a relationship whose *term* is the unity of the episcopate and
in/with/through the episcopate the unity of all the faithful,
and whose *functions* are those activities whose purpose is to
build this twofold unity, as will be explored in chapter 4.

---

11. "perpetuum utriusque unitatis principium ac visibile fundamentum"; *Pastor aeternus*, Prologus (DS 3051); Tanner, *Decrees*, 2:812.

This understanding gives a distinct cast to what is "indispensable" and what is "dispensable." At issue is not the progressive growth with its inalienable members of an organic substance, but the *ratio* of a relationship, a relationship whose term is one with its purpose and whose foundation lies in divine institution. One cannot judge dispensability simply by prior historical settlements. The more important question is how any historical strategy or embodiment emerges from its foundation and bears upon its purpose.

It could well have been necessary, for example, that the shape given to the papal ministry by Gregory VII in all of its centralizing features was dialectically necessary for the freedom of the local church from secular rulers in the electing of its bishop; while now that same centralizing dynamic is weakening the local church through an excessive focus upon the Holy See, made even more intense by the cultural changes worked through mass communications.[12] The deposition powers of the Roman Pontiff can be arguably justified at a given time in Europe for the unity of the Christian community within what was styled "Christendom," and at another time they are judged antiquated to the point of quaint. It could equally be true that the present dispositions for the appointment of bishops were indispensable for the retrieval of these appointments from the absolute nation-state, but that the time has come to return much of this power to the local churches.

---

12. William Henn, O.F.M. Cap., "Historical-Theological Synthesis of the Relation between Primacy and Episcopacy during the Second Millennium," *Il primato del successore de Pietro: Atti del simposio teologico, Roma, dicembre 1996* (Vatican City: Libreria Editrice Vaticana, 1997), 224–26; Stephan O. Horn, S.D.S., "Geschichtlich-theologische Synthese des Verhältnisses von Primat und Episkopat im ersten Jahrtausend," *Il primato del successore de Pietro: Atti del simposio teologico, Roma, dicembre 1996* (Vatican City: Libreria Editrice Vaticana, 1997), 193.

In none of these settlements is there question of retaining or denying a power that is indispensable. It is not a question of an abstract *de jure divino* or *divina institutione.* The vital question asks about a historical realization of a relationship — set up by the sacrament of episcopal consecration — through a set of functions. The Church has the freedom to take them up and to lay them down as they realize the genuine relationship of the primacy. It seems ill advised to attempt to ground any such particular embodiments on the specific choice of Christ; the ground should be that of the indispensable ministry/responsibility given to the primacy: the fostering of the unity in faith and love throughout the leadership and membership of the Church, i.e., the confirmation of the brethren. *Potestas* is for *munus,* and the *munus* is for unity.

Any doctrinal synthesis, as noted above, looks to a governing concept or a comprehensive principle in terms of which every other element takes on its constitutive meaning and its value within the whole. So much of Aquinas's treatment of the divine essence and its attributes, for example, takes as its comprehensive intelligibility the divine nature as *ipsum esse subsistens* — all arguments eventually lead back to this capacious apprehension of God. Similarly, so many of the inquiries of Karl Rahner find their foundational grounding in the mystery of the self-communication of God, the comprehensive principle that gives systematic unity to his theology.

What must function as the comprehensive principle through which the primacy is to be understood? The unity of the episcopate and, by means of that unity, the unity of the Church — a unity that is in faith and communion. This is the twofold term of the relationship that is the primacy and that gives to the primacy its character.

It goes without saying that unity does not mean uniformity. Unity means a gathering into one, and it presupposes that all of the united members are "there," conjoined in all of their individual integrity. If something of their integrity, of their uniqueness is left out or suppressed, then the unity in faith and communion is proportionally incomplete. It is this connection between the unity and integrity of the realities united that makes it possible for the present pope to move so easily between seeing the pope as a servant of unity and as one charged to strengthen his brethren. Authentic unity is impossible without the full presence of its members. The papal responsibility to unify and to strengthen will emerge even more importantly as the concept of *communio* grows and as each of the local churches is understood in this mutual reciprocity to contribute the irreplaceable manner in which it embodies the universal Church.

Vatican I had highlighted the unity that is the term of primacy — but not adequately. Its perspective on the Church is so strongly upon its universality under the Roman Pontiff that the nature of that to which the primacy is related, the episcopate and the local churches, remained undeveloped. But if the character of a relation is determined by its term, by that towards which it is a relation, then even the primacy itself is insufficiently understood after Vatican I. Primacy, the episcopate, and the faithful can only be understood together.

CHAPTER FOUR

Unity as Communion

The synod of bishops that met in 1985 gave the following judgment about the Second Vatican Council: "The ecclesiology of communion is the central and fundamental idea of the Council's documents."[1] This statement seems difficult to justify completely through a study of the actual documents of the council. Its reading of the council is rather through the "effective history" that followed the closing of the council. Its understanding of the council's documents reflects the reception of the conciliar texts into an understanding of the Church as *communio* that flourished in the theology that surrounded the council but broke into its official texts only occasionally, rising to much greater prominence in the period that immediately followed the council. Pope John Paul II signaled this ecclesiological development in the Apostolic Constitution *Sacrae disciplinae leges,* promulgating the new Code of Canon Law:

> Among the elements which characterize the true and genuine image of the Church we should emphasize especially the following: ... the doctrine in which the Church is seen as a *communion* and which therefore determines the relations

---

1. For this and similar texts together with a judgment of their accuracy, see J. Michael Miller, C.S.B., *The Shepherd and the Rock: Origins, Development and Mission of the Papacy* (Huntington, Ind.: Our Sunday Visitor Publishing Division, 1995), 216.

which are to exist between the particular churches and the universal Church, and between collegiality and the primacy.[2]

Certainly, the Second Vatican Council introduces much greater consideration of the particular churches and of their communication, but this inclusion embodies what Joseph Komonchak legitimately calls "the transitional character of the council's doctrine on the church, which the new code continues to reflect." Komonchak's judgment upon the ecclesiology of Vatican II seems sober and justified: "Not only did the council begin its work within the perspectives of the universalist ecclesiology long dominant in the West, but its recovery of an ecclesiology of communion that underlies a theology of the local church was hesitant and unsystematic."[3] The later statement of the Doctrinal Congregation seems accurate, both about the past emergence of this term and about its future promise: "The concept of *communion* (κοινωνία), which appears with a certain prominence in the texts of the Second Vatican Council, is very suitable for expressing the core of the mystery of the Church and can certainly be a key for the renewal of Catholic ecclesiology."[4] It might be said that the recovery of the centrality of *communio* for understanding the life and coherence of the Church received its impetus during the Second Vatican Council and

---

2. John Paul II, *Sacrae disciplinae leges,* in *Code of Canon Law, Latin-English Edition* (Washington, D.C.: Canon Law Society of America, 1983), xv.

3. Joseph A. Komonchak, "The Local Church and the Church Catholic: The Contemporary Theological Problematic," *The Jurist* 52 (1992): 427.

4. Congregation for the Doctrine of the Faith, *Letter to the Bishops of the Catholic Church on Some Aspects of the Church Understood as Communion* (Rome: reprinted by the United States Catholic Conference, 1992), Introduction. It is interesting to note where the Congregation finds this concept, *communio,* emerging during the council. It cites: *Lumen gentium,* nos. 4, 8, 13–15, 18, 21, 24–25; *Dei verbum,* no. 10; *Gaudium et spes,* no. 32; *Unitatis redintegratio,* nos. 2–4, 14–15, 17–19, 22.

its steady development after the council — not unlike in this the progressive introduction of the vernacular into the liturgy of the Western Church.

This recovery was a critically important moment of retrieval from the very beginnings of the Church. Klaus Schatz has written:

> The key to the ancient Church's self-understanding is the word *communio* [communion]. It encompasses varied dimensions: first of all, the *communio* is the local church as a community of believers with the bishop as its center. Beyond that, it is the communion of faith uniting the churches with one another. This includes not only Eucharistic communion, but also the very important element of communication.[5]

During the council perhaps the finest depiction of the Church as communion emerged in *Unitatis redintegratio*:

> For many centuries, the churches of the east and the west followed their separate ways though linked in a *brotherly communion* [*fraterna communione*] of faith and sacramental life; the Roman see by common consent acted as guide when disagreements arose between them over matters of faith and discipline.

And the Decree on Ecumenism praises the faithful of the East because of their care and concern "to preserve the communion in faith and charity" (*in fidei caritatisque communione*) "which ought to exist between local churches, as between sisters."[6] *Communio* offers a new understanding of the unity of the Church because, paradoxically, it is a retrieval of a patristic understanding of the Church as a *communio ecclesiarum*.

---

5. Klaus Schatz, *Papal Primacy: From Its Origins to the Present*, trans. John A. Otto and Linda M. Maloney (Collegeville, Minn.: Liturgical Press, 1996), 17.

6. *Unitatis redintegratio*, no. 14; Tanner, *Decrees*, 2:916 (m).

This understanding begins with the universal Church as actualized among or within particular peoples with particular histories and cultures and in particular places. The Church does not become universal by binding into federation these local churches. The universal Church is not the sum of the local churches. The local church is the Church universal as it is present and operative and actualized in this particular place and culture. If it is not the universal Church, it is not the Church at all; it is a sect.[7] These churches are not bound by federation, but by the common sharing of those principles that constitute and generate the Church, those sources of communion that Komonchak — following Vatican II — lists as the call of God, the Word of Christ, the grace of the Spirit, the Eucharist, the apostolic ministry.[8] One local church recognizes another as it recognizes itself, and in that recognition the ontic universality of the Church — that must be present in any authentic presence of the Church — comes into ontological consciousness. The one Church, which is universally the sacrament of salvation for all human beings, is this communion of particular or local churches, and achieves actualization only in and through these particular churches.[9] In such an understanding of the Church, the term of the relationship that is the primacy is apprehended not so much as simply the unity of the Church, whether of episcopate or the faithful, as it is the communion of the churches, realized among the bishops who represent these churches and among the faithful who constitute them.

---

7. For the origins of this important distinction between church and sect used somewhat differently, see Ernst Troeltsch, *The Social Teaching of the Christian Churches*, trans. Olive Wyon (New York: Harper and Brothers, 1960), 2:993.

8. Komonchak, "The Local Church and the Church Catholic," 421–22.

9. *Lumen gentium*, no. 23; Tanner, *Decrees*, 2:867.

Crucial as is this apostolic ministry, both primacy and episcopacy, for the unity of the Church, it remains instrumental. The primordial and fundamental source of unity or communion is the Holy Spirit, the Spirit given by the risen Christ and communicated through sacrament and word throughout the Church, drawing into communion the people of God and configuring in them the fullness of Christ, and so moving within the Church as to constitute the apostolic ministries by which it is efficaciously present. The Spirit of Christ is what the Church most profoundly shares, and it is this sharing that constitutes its deepest communion.[10]

It seems accurate to say, then, that "unity" as predicated of the Church and the churches is being seen increasingly in this way, that is, as communion. One can notice that the two terms have become interchangeable. So the Doctrinal Congregation wrote in 1992: "It is possible to apply the concept of communion *in analogous fashion* to the union existing among particular Churches and to see the universal Church as a communion of Churches."[11] Again, the two terms are treated as interchangeable: "Unity, or communion between the particular Churches in the universal Church, is rooted..."[12]

Communio advances the notion of "unity" into a much more dynamic understanding. For *communio* can denote (1) either the activities and passivities, the vital interactions of word and sacrament, of pastoral care and teaching, of compassion and charity that are the effects and signs of the Spirit as its dwells within and defines the Church or (2) the relationships or communities founded on these activities that are the local churches. For the primacy to have as its term the communion of the churches, the communion of communions,

---

10. See *Lumen gentium,* no. 4; Tanner, *Decrees,* 2:850; no. 13; Tanner, *Decrees,* 2:859; *Unitatis redintegratio,* no. 2; Tanner, *Decrees,* 2:909.

11. *Church Understood as Communion,* no. 8.

12. *Church Understood as Communion,* no. 11.

is still to have its character given by the unity that it serves, but unity conceived dynamically and with all of the internal and rich diversity that "Catholic" implies. The Roman see is seen in such an ecclesiology, as Stephan Horn traces out the first millennium, to be the *Zentrum der Communio.*[13]

This retrieval and development of *communio* opens up to still another understanding of the promise and of the responsibilities of the primacy: the fostering of the unity among the Christian churches and ecclesial communities, the ecumenical dimension of the papal *munus.* Increasingly, the pope has taken a central position in service of the movements towards Christian unity. The most recent encyclical, *Ut unum sint,* bears witness to this concern in a manner that would have been unthinkable forty years ago. The dialogues with other Christian confessions have disclosed Christian communities more open to the possibility of a universal primacy that would foster this extended *communio* — open to this primacy in a manner equally unprecedented. *Communio* as the unity proper to the particular churches and as the dynamic unity that is the term of the *munus* of the papal primacy is bringing into focus ecumenical possibilities whose outlines as yet one can only dimly see. It can be safely asserted that in the gradual evolution of a deeper communion among the Christian churches and ecclesial communions, one of the great Catholic contributions will be this ministry of the bishop of Rome.

Where "unity" is employed in the rest of this book, it must be understood in the fuller sense given it in the period during and following Vatican II, that is, it will be used in the sense of "communion."

---

13. Stephan O. Horn, S.D.S., "Geschichtlich-theologische Synthese des Verhältnisses von Primat und Episkopat im ersten Jahrtausend," *Il primato del successore de Pietro: Atti del simposio teologico, Roma, dicembre 1996* (Vatican City: Libreria Editrice Vaticana, 1997), 193ff.

CHAPTER FIVE

The Episcopal Character
of Papal Primacy

If the episcopate, precisely in its unity in faith and communion, is one term of the relationship that is the primacy, then is the subject of that relationship also episcopal? Is the *munus* of the primacy also an episcopal *munus*, albeit a specialized one and one exercised from within the college of bishops? Is it from within the episcopate that the episcopate itself is supported and fostered in its unity?

The overwhelming weight of tradition in its attribution of the primacy to the bishop of Rome as such and the more recent and authoritative declarations of the Apostolic See indicate that the pope exercises the primacy precisely as bishop of Rome, as a member of the episcopate; the primacy denotes a *munus* that is genuinely episcopal. Primacy among the bishops comes to this bishop because of his see, the see of Rome.

This episcopal character of the primacy was explicitly stated during the First Vatican Council, by Bishop Zinelli, representing the Deputation of Faith in his reply to Bishop Dupanloup on July 5, 1870. He placed the pope in his primacy within the episcopal college:

> It must be admitted that the power of the sovereign pontiff is in reality [*realiter*] of the same type as that of the bishops [*esse eandem speciem ac potestatem episcoporum*]. Why then not use the same word to describe the quality of jurisdiction

exercised by popes and by bishops, and why not say that
the episcopal power resides in the bishops and the supreme
episcopal power in the sovereign pontiff?[1]

Consequently, *Pastor aeternus* qualifies the ordinary and
immediate papal power of jurisdiction as *vere episcopalis*.[2]

That the *munus* of the primacy is an episcopal *munus* runs
insistently like a leitmotiv through the recent encyclical *Ut
unum sint*:

> This service of unity, rooted in the action of divine mercy, is
> entrusted *within* the college of bishops to one among those
> who have received from the Spirit the task, not of exercising
> power over the people — as the rulers of the gentiles and their
> great men do (cf. Matt. 20:25; Mark 10:42) — but of leading
> them toward peaceful pastures.[3]

The Catholic Church

> does not separate this office from the mission entrusted to
> the whole body of bishops, who are also "vicars and ambas-
> sadors of Christ" (*Lumen gentium*, no. 27). The bishop of
> Rome is a member of the "college" and the bishops are his
> brothers in the ministry.[4]

The episcopal character of the primacy obviously connects
the primacy and the episcopate much more closely. The primacy not only has the episcopate for its term; the primacy is
also a special relationship that emerges from within the episcopate. It is an instrumentality by which the episcopate cares
for its own unity — and consequently its own existence —
in the meaning of the Gospel and the fidelity of its life according to the Gospel. Further, when the pope cares for and

---

1. Mansi 52, 1104. For this text, see J. M. R. Tillard, O.P., *The Bishop
of Rome*, trans. John de Satgé (Wilmington, Del.: Michael Glazier, 1983),
143. This essay is very much in debt to the work of Father Tillard.

2. *Pastor aeternus*, chap. 3 (DS 3060); Tanner, *Decrees*, 2:814.

3. *Ut unum sint*, no. 94, in *AAS* 87:11 (November 10, 1995): 976–77.
ET: *Origins* 25, no. 4 (June 8, 1995): 69; emphasis added.

4. *Ut unum sint*, no. 95, in *AAS*, 977–78; *Origins*, 69.

fosters the unity of the Church, he is embodying uniquely the care of the entire episcopate for the unity of the Church. *Pastor aeternus,* in its initial paragraphs, asserts that the union of bishops among themselves, the unity of the episcopate — there included as *sacerdotes* — effects the unity of the faithful among themselves. Then the papal *munus* towards the entire Church is a unique realization of the *munus* of the college of bishops as a whole.

The primacy, then, relates to the episcopate in at least three ways: the primacy fosters the unity of the episcopate in faith and communion; the primacy emerges from within the episcopal college as a *munus* proper to a particular member of the episcopate; the primacy embodies the care of the entire episcopate for the unity of all the faithful. The primacy is in service to the episcopate; and the episcopate, including the primacy, is in service to the faithful. This position concurs with that of Karl Rahner: "The primacy of the pope is a primacy *within* and not *vis-à-vis* this college."[5]

---

5. Karl Rahner, "On the Divine Right of the Episcopate," *The Episcopate and the Primacy,* 77–78.

Chapter Six

The Functions of the Papal Primacy: Habitual and Substitutional

If the *munus* of the Petrine office bears upon a unity among the members of the episcopate in faith and love, and if that *munus* is generically the same as that of the bishops themselves, what are its functions? How does it accomplish its divine mission?

The First Vatican Council condemns those who would restrict this function to

> merely an office of inspection and guidance, and not [assent to] the full and supreme power of jurisdiction over the whole Church and this not only in matters of faith and morals, but also in those which concern the discipline and government of the Church dispersed throughout the whole world.[1]

But to say that the papal ministry to the unity both of the episcopate and of the members of the Church demands this range of power for its adequate execution is not to assert that each use of this power is of equal weight and frequency. There are some usages that must always be present

---

1. "... tantummodo officium inspectionis vel directionis, non autem plenam et supremam potestatem iurisdictionis in universam Ecclesiam, non solum in rebus, quae ad fidem et mores, sed etiam in iis, quae ad disciplinam et regimen Ecclesiae per totum orbem diffusae pertinent" (*Pastor aeternus,* chap. 3 [DS 3064]; Tanner, *Decrees,* 2:814 [m]).

and active; there are others that exceptional circumstances evoke into operation, interventions called for by crises in the Church in which the powers of the pope must be brought to bear if the unity of the Church is to be maintained. All of these usages of the power of the primacy are equally "ordinary" in the sense that they are not delegated; but they are not equally usual nor should they be.

Peter Hünermann traces such a distinction to the German bishops in their celebrated rejoinder to the statement issued by Bismarck dated May 14, 1872, which contended that *Pastor aeternus* in ascribing *potestas suprema, ordinaria et immediata* to the Roman Pontiff had effectively absorbed all episcopal jurisdiction into papal jurisdiction. As Hünermann outlined the response of the German bishops: "The German bishops answered with a description of the papal functions: They are (1) in essential things, the right of the pope to the supervision of the bishops, and (2) in extraordinary circumstances, a right to intervention in the dioceses."[2] The explicit and public approval of the pope came hard on the heels of this German declaration: "Your corporate declaration is marked by clarity and exactness so that it leaves nothing to be desired.... Your declaration gives the pure Catholic doctrine and therefore that of the Holy Council and the Holy See."[3]

---

2. "Die deutschen Bischöfe antworteten mit einer Umschreibung der päpstlichen Funktionen: Es sind (1) im wesenlichen das Aufsichtsrecht des Papstes über die Bischöfe und (2) ein Eingriffsrecht in die Diözesen bei außergewöhnlichen Umständen" (Peter Hünermann, "Amt und Evangelium," *Herder Korrespondenz* [1996]: 300; numeration added). The response of the bishops is dated March of 1875. For the actual text of the German bishops, see DS 3112–16. Hünermann regrets that this differentiation and specification of the various functions of the primacy was not picked up by Vatican II.

3. For the papal response, see DS 3117; the complete text is found in J. M. R. Tillard, O.P., *The Bishop of Rome*, trans. John de Satgé (Wilmington, Del.: Michael Glazier, 1983), 140–41.

Following the lead of Yves Simon, one can then draw
a differentiation between "habitual" and "substitutional"
functions: those that obtain in the normal execution of papal
responsibilities; those that obtain in extraordinary circumstances when other structures of leadership and service have
broken down and the unity in faith and communion of
the episcopate or the faithful is severely threatened.[4] Such
a differentiation does not derogate from any aspect of the
jurisdiction of the Roman Pontiff nor does it deny the ordinary (i.e., non-delegated) and immediate ability to intervene.
But it does indicate that some of these powers are for the habitual or usual government of the Church and to be in play
during any healthy period of the Church, and that others of
these powers are provided for emergencies and crises when
the more usual practices have collapsed and the pope must
intervene.

Substitutional authority (i.e., the substitutional use of authority) is made necessary by deficiency and immaturity. It is
indispensable at a period when a local church cannot direct
itself adequately. In contrast, the habitual or essential use of
authority does not argue to immaturity on the part of those
under this authority; it rather presumes a common good of
all parties, units, and component societies in this *communio*

---

4. Yves R. Simon, *The Philosophy of Democratic Government* (Chicago: University of Chicago Press, 1951), 7–11. Obviously Simon's
distinction is here being adapted to another situation. Simon actually distinguishes between substitutional, essential, and most essential uses of
authority, the last being the direct care for the common good. This essay reduces them to two: substitutional and habitual. For the foundational
need for authority, see Thomas Aquinas, *Summa theologiae*, I. 96. 4:
"There can be no social life for a multitude unless someone presides whose
intention [*intenderet*] is for a common good. For many persons *per se* are
inclined [*intendunt*] towards many things; one, however, is inclined to one.
And so the Philosopher says (*Pol.* 1.2 1254a28) that whenever many are
ordered to one thing, it will always be found that one is principal and
directing."

and recognizes that there is someone who cares for this. One can call this habitual use of authority "essential," as does Simon, because it must be present if the primacy is present; it is essentially present. This is not true of the substitutional use of authority.

The essential or habitual character of papal primacy is obvious: the bishops are not addressed by the pope as his children, but as his brothers. The habitual use of primatial authority is to foster the unity of his brothers, not of his children — a unity in their faith and mutual charity — and with his brothers in college the unity of their churches and of the entire Church. This is not a substitutional use of authority, but an essential one, supervising the direction of developed and free human beings and particular churches towards the common good of that *communio* that is of all the churches.

Hence another way to style these two different uses of primatial authority would be to distinguish between the fraternal use and the "paternal." Simon speaks of the substitutional as the "paternal" function of authority, using "paternal" in a very specific meaning. It responds as a parent to a child that needs direction. Like the wise direction of the child by the parent, the substitutional use of authority aims at its own disappearance. If used when it is not required, it can inhibit or even injure the growth and the life of the very one it attempts to aid.

The fraternal use of papal authority would be habitual, presupposing no undue incapacity of the particular churches, but the function of the bishop of Rome to judge and oversee for the common good. The "paternal" use of authority presupposes that either at this time or in this issue, a particular church or churches are not mature enough to deal with the issues that confront them and that they need the influence of the Apostolic See to steady and support them in the responsibilities that have fallen upon them. Again, the fraternal concern of the bishop of Rome must always be present; the "paternal" use of his power would be called into play when the particular church does not have the resources to handle its own affairs for its own good and the general good of the Church. Once more, it must be stressed that all of these powers are found in the range of the bishop of Rome, but that the term of the relationship — i.e., the unity in faith and communion among the particular churches involved — dictates which of these are appropriately brought into operation.

Still another way of locating the tradition behind this terminological difference in the use of *sacra potestas* is suggested by the principle of subsidiarity, a principle that Pius XII made the differentiation between humane government and totalitarianism.[5] One cannot develop the issue of subsidiarity here, but simply refer to the study of Joseph Komonchak on the significance of this theme within the teaching of the Church.[6]

Ut unum sint takes up again the doctrine of the German declaration and specifies within this range that which is of central importance to the *munus* of the bishop of Rome: supervision. "The mission of the bishop of Rome within the college of all the pastors consists precisely in 'keeping watch' [*episkopein*]." It is this function that is subsequently specified in that same encyclical:

> [The pope] is the first servant of unity. This primacy is exercised on various levels, including vigilance over the handing down of the word, the celebration of the liturgy and the sacraments, the Church's mission, discipline and the Chris-

---

5. Pius XII, "Discourse to the Newly Created Cardinals," February 20, 1946, *AAS* 38:5 (April 1, 1946): 144–45; ET: *The Catholic Mind* 44 (April 1946): 196.

6. Joseph Komonchak, "Subsidiarity in the Church: The State of the Question," *The Jurist* 48, no. 2 (1988): 326ff.

tian life. It is the responsibility of the successor of Peter to recall the requirements of the common good of the Church, should anyone be tempted to overlook it in the pursuit of personal interests. He has the duty to admonish, to caution and to declare at times that this or that opinion being circulated is irreconcilable with the unity of faith. When circumstances require it, he speaks in the name of all the pastors in communion with him. He can also — under very specific conditions clearly laid down by the First Vatican Council — declare *ex cathedra* that a certain doctrine belongs to the deposit of faith [DS 3074]. By thus bearing witness to the truth, he serves unity.[7]

Ut unum sint locates the fundamental ministry of the primacy not in a universal administration, but in oversight or supervision or guardianship. This specification of the functions of the primacy may well make *Ut unum sint* the most constructive contribution to the understanding of the primacy and the episcopate since the council.

Peter Hünermann maintains that this encyclical opens for the Church and for the ecumenical dialogue a new situation:

> For the first time in a Roman document, the Petrine ministry of the bishop of Rome has been described in terms of its most important episcopal functions.... Fundamentally, the pope's task is characterized by the word *episkopein,* and more closely interpreted as an office of guardianship.... The primacy is characterized in the same manner.... The concept of *episkopē* would allow one to ascribe to the pope the task of keeping an eye on the respective individual authorities in the Church as they carry out their functions of safeguarding and expounding the faith. If he should see himself obliged to intervene, then, this would entail explicit respect for these other authorities and their involvement.[8]

---

7. *Ut unum sint,* no. 94, in *AAS,* 976–77; *Origins,* 69. The Latin term translated as "keeping watch" is *vigilare.*

8. Peter Hünermann, "Towards a New Unity," *The Tablet* (July 13, 1996): 916–17. He comments further that "this kind of integration of the

Both the habitual and substitutional papal functions, if they
are distinguished and brought into play when appropriate, are easily integrated into the concerns of *Pastor aeternus* and subsequent, variant statements of the magisterium
for the papal ministry towards unity in faith and communion. The distinction of the uses of primatial authority
allows the proper autonomy of the individual bishops and
of the episcopate itself to remain. Even more, it allows for
both of these to realize the directions of Jesus to Peter:
"to strengthen his brothers [στήρισον τοὺς ἀδελφούς σου]"
(Luke 22:32). It is interesting to note that of all the Petrine
texts, this one from Luke seems most often cited by the
present pope.

(Because of the limitations of time and space, this essay
must prescind from an enormously important but very complicated issue: whether the present use of primatial power by
the Roman Pontiff can and should be distinguished into that
primacy that is God's gift to His worldwide Church and that
use of authority which comes to the bishop of Rome precisely as patriarch of the West. But, while prescinding from
this question, it can be isolated as one of those issues that fall
under the rubrics of a doctrinal element which today would
merit further study.)

To grasp the importance of the episcopal nature of the
primacy and the differentiation of the habitual from the
substitutional uses of authority, one could take as a point
of departure a *sententia* from a source that one would antecedently expect to mark off a radically contrasting pole
in any discussion of the episcopate and the primacy. This
comes from a distinguished Orthodox theologian, Stylianos
Harkianakis:

---

papal magisterium within the framework of the universal Church would
make a change of current Roman practice necessary."

The question of whether the Roman primacy, formulated as it was at the First Vatican Council and also, unfortunately, at the Second, can have a place at all in...[Orthodox ecclesiology]...must be answered with an unqualified negative. This does not, however, mean rejecting the idea of a primacy within Orthodoxy. On the contrary, recognizing the ideas of synodality and collegiality leads directly towards recognizing one bishop as the first among the bishops, that is, to attribute the primacy to him; never, however, in the sense of "supreme pontiff" but always as "first among equals." When the bishop of Rome understood his primacy in the sense of *primus inter pares,* he had the possibility of expressing a decisive opinion in questions of concern to the whole Church and of being respected by all; he was thus able to provide effectively a service essential to the whole Church. But as soon as he started to understand his own episcopal power as fundamentally different from the power of all other bishops, he forfeited the possibility of being in communion with Orthodoxy....When the pope bases his power on the Petrine succession and not on the common apostolic and episcopal succession, he cuts himself off not only from the communion of bishops but also from that of the whole Church....It is therefore not for constitutional and canonical reasons only that the synodical structure of the church is so dear to the Orthodox; profoundly soteriological factors are involved. Both kinds of reason, always inter-related in Orthodox thought, combine to exclude categorically the Roman primacy of jurisdiction and infallibility.[9]

But the question must be asked: if one looks beneath the use of such language as "supreme" and beyond the historical memories that such language evokes and if one further allows for papal jurisdiction understood as fundamentally *episkopein* and distinguished between habitual and substitutional, quite honestly how actually far apart are the positions

---

9. Tillard, *The Bishop of Rome,* 5–6.

articulated by Msgr. Zinelli[10] and Stylianos Harkianakis? This does not suggest in any way that the two positions coincide, but rather that the difference between them may not be as absolute as it appears at first blush.

Both admit that the power of the bishop of Rome is episcopal, therefore of the same sacramental equality as that of other bishops — one residential bishop is not more bishop than another — whatever one says about the further intensification of this care for the Church. Can *pares* not be legitimately invoked here as indicating that what is present is episcopal, that in what is most significant, the effect of the sacrament, all are equal? The difference, then, must be one of specification and of degree. They are not simply equal; one is *primus*. Primacy entails a responsibility to and for the Church that — while the same generically as that of the entire episcopate — differs in the manner and the object upon which it is brought to bear. The pope's responsibility, in the context of Vatican I, is called *supreme*. But how vastly different is this from saying that he is *primus?* Or is there something above or beyond *primus?* How much of this problem is that of language? *Pares* in being episcopal; *primus* in being primatial.

Harkianakis even further allows the papal primacy "the possibility of expressing a decisive opinion in questions of concern to the whole Church...able to provide effectively a service essential to the whole Church." This again does not eliminate a difference, but it does significantly narrow it beyond what the initial language would seem to allow. The same analysis of language could be conducted on the meaning of "primacy of honor." Neither in the churches of the East nor in ancient Rome was *honor,* or τιμή, reduced to external reverence without significant authority. It is again

---

10. See p. 59.

not immediately obvious that the linguistic difficulties are as absolute as they have been taken to be.[11]

Can this differentiation between *pares* and *primus* be drawn in terms of orders and jurisdiction (even though, as Henn notes, this distinction does not obtain in the Eastern churches and even though in the West in the Catholic Church since Vatican II "to the extent that the order-jurisdiction distinction concerned the ability to 'exercise' episcopal ministry, it would appear that the expression 'hierarchical communion' has taken its place")?[12] But if it is to be employed here, it would appear that in orders, i.e., sacramentally, all bishops are equal — *pares;* but in jurisdiction, the bishop of Rome possesses a unique authority — as in their own more limited ways do the patriarchs and the metropolitans. He is *primus* in this twofold strengthening of his brethren. But he is not alone. The college of bishops possesses that same responsibility. And to a lesser and more limited way, so do each of the bishops. The difference here seems one of degree in the intensity and range of the *munus regendi.* The question can then be legitimately raised: does not the very ambiguous phrase *primus inter pares* also admit of a sense that is unobjectionable for Catholic theology, one that weighs *primus* heavily enough to justify the use of the term at all? There is at least one Catholic theologian who has answered this question in the affirmative.[13]

At present, it must be admitted that what Vatican I meant

11. Brian E. Daley, S.J. "Position and Patronage in the Early Church: The Original Meaning of 'Primacy of Honour,'" *Journal of Theological Studies* 44, no. 2 (October 1993): 529–53.

12. William Henn, O.F.M. Cap., "Historical-Theological Synthesis of the Relation between Primacy and Episcopacy during the Second Millennium," *Il primato del successore de Pietro: Atti del simposio teologico, Roma, dicembre 1996* (Vatican City: Libreria Editrice Vaticana, 1997), 258.

13. Tillard, *The Bishop of Rome,* 115, 157.

by "supreme" is indeed vastly different from what Harkianakis means by *primus*. Even to find a sense for *primus inter pares* that is unobjectionable for Catholic theology is by no means to come upon a meaning that would necessarily be acceptable to the Orthodox. But perhaps the ambiguous phrase does suggest a step forward. Cooperative Orthodox and Catholic studies could be engaged to determine — insofar as this is possible — what the primacy of the see of Rome meant to the Eastern bishops during the first millennium. This in turn might suggest further steps as possible.

Repeatedly it is asserted that of the "pair primacy-episcopacy, it is difficult to emphasize the authority of the one without in some way apparently or effectively diminishing the authority of the other."[14] Historically, this has certainly been true and the internal tension and even dialectical history have been well narrated by William Henn. But there is something curiously paradoxical about such a history. If a central purpose of the papacy is the confirmation of the episcopate in its own faith and life of charity, then the primacy is rightly understood and correctly executed if and to the degree that it unites and strengthens the episcopate in faith and communion. It is the strength and unity of the episcopate that indicates the strength and effectiveness of the primacy. A papacy that would actually weaken the legitimate powers of the bishops has become seriously disordered. Primacy is not the same as predominance, and it could as well be realized authentically in a diminishment of dominance as in its increase.

That is why it seems important to see the primacy categorically as a relationship given its character by its term. The primacy is to foster the communion of the episcopate in faith and charity — the episcopate in all its fullness, nothing left

---

14. Henn, "Historical-Theological Synthesis," 232.

out or suppressed or negated or omitted. As the episcopate is strengthened in its full life and as this vital episcopate is sustained in its unity, authentic primacy is present. Do the fears of the Orthodox count against such an understanding and practice of primacy? It is not evident that they must. Certainly all would agree, Catholics as well as Orthodox, that a primacy that would not confirm the episcopate in its fullness, that would turn bishops into *de facto* papal functionaries, would not be a primacy, but a predominance that has become injurious.

It is critical to note also that the principal and unifying service of the primacy to the unity of the Church does not lie in any particular acts of its supervision or guardianship — important as these are. It is rather in its symbolism: what the primacy embodies and manifests. It is a rich and effective symbolism devolving from its history and functions, and it has a most telling effect not only upon the bishops, but upon the entire worldwide Church. Any Church leader is necessarily a symbol of unity, the pastor for his parish and the bishop for his diocese. *De facto*, the pope, as no other figure or group, represents in the Catholic imagination and symbolic life the communion that is the Church. For many outside the Catholic Church, the pope has come to stand for the presence and the voice of Christianity.

This is not, nor should it be allowed to become confused with, a cult of personality; in many ways, this ecclesial symbolism is the opposite of a cult of personality. It is a recognition of what the primacy embodies: the care for the communion of the churches. The concrete historical figure of the pope is — by what he is — a constant call for deeper communion and self-recognition among the members of the Church, summoning each of the particular churches beyond national consciousness and local histories to a care for the Church in its worldwide extension. It is simply a fact that the pope constitutes such a sign of the unity within the whole Church. In the many functions and uses of papal authority, habitual and substitutional, this character of the papacy is disclosed; and that character is fundamentally a call, even an efficacious symbol, for the communion that is the Church.

This chapter has been a consideration of the relationship between the primacy and the episcopate, and of the Church as a whole only insofar as it is served by this relationship. But it must be said that the primary relationship of the bishop of Rome as one who continues the Petrine ministry is to the unity of the whole Church with the unity of bishops, a part of the Church, as instrumental to this communion of all the faithful. These few paragraphs are only to note that the pope ministers to this unity also symbolically — not simply by teaching or administration, but by being what he is.

CHAPTER SEVEN

From Episcopate to Collegiality

The Gospels recognize the progressive development among those who followed Jesus. Jesus gathers disciples around himself. From these, he selects the Twelve, called "apostles" in the Synoptic Gospels (Matt. 10:2–4; Mark 3:14–19; Luke 6:13–16). These are subsequently given powers as a group for their mission. It is of the Twelve that Jesus asks the question about His identity. It is this question addressed in the plural to the Twelve that Peter answers (Matt. 16:15–16), a spokesmanship role for which he is not corrected by Jesus or by the Twelve and which is mentioned as such in *Ut unum sint*. There can be no real question about the priority of Peter among the Twelve, but they are all bound in a collegial unity. As *Ut unum sint* summarizes the biblical evidence:

> The first part of the Acts of the Apostles presents Peter as the one who speaks in the name of the apostolic group and who serves the unity of the community — all the while respecting the authority of James, the head of the church in Jerusalem. The function of Peter must continue in the Church so that under its sole head, who is Jesus Christ, it may be visibly present in the world as the communion of all his disciples.[1]

---

1. "Prima pars Actuum Apostolorum ostendit Petrum tamquam *loquentem nomine coetus apostolici* et servientem unitati communitatis — idque dum observat auctoritatem Iacobi, praepositi Ecclesiae Hierosolymitanae. Hoc officium Petri in Ecclesia permanere debet ut, sub uno suo Capite, qui est Christus Iesus, ipsa in mundo visibiliter communio sit cunctorum eius disciplorum" (*Ut unum sint*, no. 97, in *AAS*, 978–79; *Origins*, 70 [m]; italics added).

Peter speaks as spokesman for the apostolic college, and it is this function that is to be preserved in the Church. The structure prior to that of its authoritative spokesman is obviously that of the college of apostles. William Henn from his analysis of *Lumen gentium,* nos. 19–24, has noted that "the idea of an episcopal college is the framework within which Vatican II wishes to describe not only the sacramental nature of the episcopacy but also the relation between the episcopacy and the primacy of the pope."[2] In doing so, the council develops further the understanding of primatial power as *vere episcopalis.*

In the nuanced manner that the pope is the successor of Peter, so the college of bishops is to be successor of the apostolic college in its rule within the Church.[3] One must recognize that just as the primacy of Peter arises from within the college of apostles and serves that college in leadership and confirmation, so the college of apostles arises from within all the disciples — those who follow Christ, who will be over the centuries named "Christians" and who are called "the people of God" in *Lumen gentium* — and serves the full ecclesial community. If a term of the primacy is the unity or communion proper to the bishops, collegiality takes on a special meaning vis-à-vis the primacy: to foster collegiality among the bishops is a purpose of the primacy and a gauge of its success.

"Collegiality" itself is newly arrived on the scene of theological discourse. The noun is an abstraction that indicates the relation inhering in each bishop by which each is ori-

---

2. William Henn, O.F.M. Cap., "Historical-Theological Synthesis of the Relation between Primacy and Episcopacy during the Second Millennium," *Il primato del successore de Pietro: Atti del simposio teologico, Roma, dicembre 1996* (Vatican City: Libreria Editrice Vaticana, 1997), 256.

3. *Lumen gentium,* nos. 21–22; Tanner, *Decrees,* 2:865–67.

ented individually towards all of the other bishops in the college of bishops and collectively in their common responsibility for the entire Church. Michael Fahey calculates that in *Lumen gentium* and *Christus Dominus* the episcopate is seen as a "college" some thirty-seven times, and the relations within the episcopate are styled as "collegial" some fifteen times. Other words figure synonymously with "collegium": *ordo, corpus,* and *fraternitas.*[4] The development from *Pastor aeternus* to *Lumen gentium,* from speaking of the bishops as the episcopate to speaking of the bishops as "a college...or a college of bishops" (*collegium...seu corpus episcoporum*), is far more considerable than a simple semantic shift. "Episcopate" is somewhat more abstract than the "college of bishops," and it fails to express the dynamic relationship of the bishops among themselves. *Collegium* obviously denotes a relationship, as do *ordo, corpus,* and *fraternitas,* and the determination about the college of bishops Hervé Legrand notes as "the most animated debate of the entire last council."[5]

The Second Vatican Council determined the *actions* by which one is established in this relationship: "A person is constituted a member of the episcopal body by virtue of sacramental consecration and by hierarchical communion with the head and members of the college."[6] Sacramental consecration and hierarchical communion are the foundation for the relationship that is episcopacy. The council also de-

---

4. Michael A. Fahey, "Collegiality," *The HarperCollins Encyclopedia of Catholicism,* ed. Richard P. McBrien (San Francisco: Harper, 1995), 329a–b.

5. Hervé Legrand, "Collégialité des évêques et communion des églises dans la recéption de Vatican II," *Revue des sciences philosophiques et théologiques* 75 (October 1991): 545.

6. "Membrum corporis episcopalis aliquis constituitur vi sacramentalis consecrationis et hierarchica communione cum collegii capite atque membris" (*Lumen gentium,* no. 22; Tanner, *Decrees,* 2:866).

termined the *potestas* that this college receives: "The order of bishops, which succeeds the college of apostles in teaching authority and pastoral government, and indeed in which the apostolic body continues to exist without interruption, is also the subject of supreme and full power over the universal Church, provided it remains united with its head, the Roman pontiff, and never without its head; and this power can be exercised only with the consent of the Roman pontiff."[7] This equates the power of the college of bishops with that of the primacy.

Now if the pope is to foster the unity or communion among the bishops in faith and charity, and through this the unity or communion of the churches, then it is clear that the pope must foster the vitality and interaction and functions of the college of bishops, of which he is the head. The primacy is to serve collegiality, just as collegiality is to serve the Church. Primacy is not opposed to collegiality in principle; on the contrary, primacy is the servant of collegiality. Further, one can gauge the effectiveness of the primacy by the vitality of collegiality within the Church. If the college of bishops is flourishing — a college precisely of bishops with and under the bishop of Rome and not merely of advisors of the Apostolic See and implementers of curial decisions — then the primacy is flourishing. This strength of bishops as bishops is a term and a reason for the primacy.

If, however, they are *de facto* taken as opposed, as they were by an influential number during the debates at the

---

7. "Ordo autem episcoporum, qui collegio apostolorum in magisterio et regimine pastorali succedit, immo in quo corpus apostolicum continuo perseverat, una cum capite suo Romano pontifice, et numquam sine hoc capite, subiectum quoque supremae ac plenae potestatis in universam ecclesiam existit, quae quidem potestas nonnisi consentiente Romano pontifice exerceri potest" (*Lumen gentium,* no. 22; Tanner, *Decrees,* 2:866).

Second Vatican Council, or if the strength of one were to be counted as the weakness of the other, then the primacy could only be less than successful in one of its essential ministries.[8] What was to be an instrument of collegiality would be read as its adversary. In that situation, the very head of the college would feel threatened by it. But the opposite is the case. A primacy that does not strengthen the college of bishops precisely as such would fail to realize the primacy taught by either Vatican Council. It would rather become domination, actually destructive of the vigor of the episcopate and of the life of local churches by its excessive centralization.

This crucially important supportive relationship that must obtain between the primacy and the episcopate is not an insight that burst upon the world with Vatican II. *Pastor aeternus,* for example, taught that the *potestas* of the Supreme Pontiff was not in opposition to that of the bishops, but rather supportive: "this same [power of the bishops] is asserted, strengthened and defended by the supreme and universal pastor."[9] This is one of the most crucial areas that must be studied: how to achieve the relationship between episcopate and the primacy not in terms of dialectical tension, but in terms of support — such support that the contemporary papacy can echo quite authentically the claim of

---

8. Schatz describes the primary form of episcopal collegiality in the early Church: "The chief emphasis was on collegiality, as in the present-day episcopal conferences. Their principal organ was not the metropolitan, but the provincial synod. The metropolitan was essentially a *primus inter pares*, much like the president of an episcopal conference today." He notes further that by the early Middle Ages, this kind of synod had largely disappeared (*Papal Primacy: From Its Origins to the Present,* trans. John A. Otto and Linda M. Maloney [Collegeville, Minn.: Liturgical Press, 1996], 69).

9. "...eadem a supremo et universali pastore asseratur, roboretur ac vindicetur" (*Pastor aeternus,* chap. 3 [DS 3061]; Tanner, *Decrees,* 2:814).

Gregory the Great: "My honor is the steadfast strength of my brethren."[10]

By no means is that the only problem which the college of bishops initially poses. *Lumen gentium,* no. 22, did not include in its description of the episcopal college the local churches of which the bishops were shepherds and representatives. If one fails to place this section within the context of *Lumen gentium,* no. 23, one would have an understanding of the college of bishops without the simultaneous and explicit recognition of the communion of churches, indeed, without mention of the local churches at all. The perspective would remain that of a universalist ecclesiology, and the college of bishops would be read as if it were primarily a governing board of the whole Church. Similarly the new Code of Canon Law introduced the diocese or particular churches only after it had treated the bishops. Hervé Legrand has written that in the Code "the concept of the college is interpreted as a college of persons existing prior to the local churches and — so to speak — independently of them."[11] This, however, is not what the college of bishops means. Individual bishops represent their own churches, and through their union in college the *communio ecclesiarum* is both symbolized and effected.

If the primacy is a relationship whose terms are in various ways the unity of the episcopal college and the unity of the people of God — variantly realized in college and in communication — episcopate is a relationship whose terms are

---

10. "Meus honor est fratrum meorum solidus vigor" (Gregory I, *Letter to Eulogius of Alexandria, Monumenta Germaniae Historica,* Ep. 2, 31/28–30; PL 77:933C; cited in *Pastor aeternus* [DS 3061]; Tanner, *Decrees,* 2:814).

11. "Le concept de collège est interprété comme un collège de personnes existant préalablement aux Églises locales et pour ainsi dire indépendamment d'elles" (Legrand, "Collégialité," 548–49).

also twofold: the collectivity of bishops in college and the relationship of the bishops with the people of God. This latter involves the vital relationship between the bishop and the local church within which he is to represent the leadership and the sanctifying presence of Christ. It is in these individual churches — especially in their eucharistic celebrations — over which the bishops preside that the universal Church becomes actual. The Church does not and cannot exist apart from the local churches. Their communion constitutes the unity of the Church extended throughout the world. The bishops in college represent, foster, and actualize this *communio ecclesiarum*, which communion the *munus* of the primacy is also to foster. For it is only in and out of these particular churches that the Catholic Church exists.[12]

The supervision of the papal primacy is for the sake of episcopal communion; mediately but fundamentally, in, with, and through the college of bishops, it is for the communion of the faithful, the unity of the worldwide Church. In terms of teleology, one can perceive in these ministries a sequence of ends: first and above all, the unity/communion of the faithful in faith and charity, served by the unity/communion/collegiality of the bishops; second, this unity or college of the bishops served by the primacy. This is of paramount importance. For one must begin by thinking of the mystery that is the Church for which these ministries exist in service and in which they must be grounded, both episcopal and papal. This allows one to move from "unity" to "communion" and its actualization in the local churches. In terms of finality, as in other ways, a theology of ministry must be derived from an ecclesiology, rather than vice-versa, and this ecclesiology must consciously recognize that in the mystery of the Church, one confronts not only its unity and

---

12. *Lumen gentium*, no. 23; Tanner, *Decrees*, 2:867.

its worldwide extension in a shared faith and charity, but its actualization, above all, in the eucharistic communities. Here the Church is understood and is experienced as a communion, an event, in which the word and sacraments come into presence and give historical tangibility to God's offer of salvation and sanctification in Christ to a given people at this time and this place. "In the Eucharist, the union of the faithful with Christ and with one another is also most tangibly visible, and at the Holy Table most interiorly realized."[13] Just as the unity of the Church will ultimately engage the *munus* of primacy and episcopate, so will the vitality of the eucharistic assemblies embody the fullest actualization of the Church.

This actualization of the Church may constitute the greatest challenge of the episcopate today. To offer a concrete example: when people of obvious sincerity "leave the Church" in the United States, as often as not it is because they experience the Church as an oppressive or abstract institution rather than as a vital communion. They walk away from the Catholic Church for more evangelical communities, often for pentecostal and fundamentalist sects or for smaller groups that seem more obviously Christian in the simplicity of their life, in their investment in one another — more serious about the common praise and worship of God, more prayerful and more mutually challenging and supportive — in place of the very large, anonymous parishes of so many Catholics who find themselves living isolated and often lonely lives of faith.

The central task confronting the Church in the United States, for example, may well lie with the restoration of the particular churches — "in which and out of which," as *Lu-*

---

13. Karl Rahner, in Karl Rahner and Joseph Ratzinger, *The Episcopate and the Primacy* (New York: Herder and Herder, 1963), 25–26.

men Gentium, no. 23, teaches, the universal Church exists —
of small and genuine communities that are eucharistic communities and that range from small parishes to the more
extended dioceses.[14] For within local churches presided over
by a bishop, there is a profound need for the vitality of these
even smaller communities within which one can and does
come to experience the fullness of the Body of Christ precisely as a community: where this interchange of love and of
mutual interest is common and expected; where the Gospel
is read and discussed, preached and assimilated into life;
where the Eucharist calls to a common life and to those com-
mitments in which the Spirit of Christ is obviously present.
There is a need for the quality of episcopal leadership so that
the diocese might encourage such smaller communions and
itself become a communion of communions. What must give
direction and urgency to many different pastoral and teaching ministries of the bishop is the formation or the retrieval
of such communities that are experienced — not inferred —
to be the real presence of the Church.

For in each of these moments, the universal Church is
present — that is the only Church there is. It is the communion of the people within the Eucharist that constitutes their
life; it is the mutual recognition of these assemblies, one of
the other, that allows the Church to be seen at various ex-
tensions of its reality as a communion of communions, each
assembly recognizing itself in the other. Recognition does
not constitute universality; that is already present. Recognition captures in consciousness the fundamental universality
that must be present if the Church is present. The particular
Church that is the care of a single bishop represents in the
intercommunion of its smaller communities the greater inter-

---

14. *Lumen gentium,* no. 23; Tanner, *Decrees,* 2:867.

communion of the worldwide Church. In this way, the local or particular Church is modeled on the universal Church.[15]

Here the ministry both of the papal primacy and of the college of bishops is seen as one which fosters and intensifies in a common faith and charity the communion of these particular churches, represented in and by their bishop. The primacy and the college as such are to foster this communion of the churches as each bishop is to foster this communion within his particular Church.

The college of bishops realizes and represents in its own communion, in its collegiality of care and responsibility, the worldwide communion of the various particular churches. These churches are not simply subdivisions of the universal Church, and one cannot think of their bishops primarily as members of a prior administrative board. The Church is a *communio ecclesiarum,* and that *communio* is represented by its bishops in college. However one explains the numerous exceptions, bishops — in their prime analogue — are ordained and designated for the care of a particular Church; *ipso facto* that ordination, together with hierarchical communion, makes them members of the episcopal college. How these two relationships obtain, what their formal priority and interdependence are, constitutes another one of those questions that merit serious study.

---

15. *Lumen gentium,* no. 23; Tanner, *Decrees,* 2:867.

CHAPTER EIGHT

Primacy, Episcopate, and the Local Churches

There are, of course, many other issues that an essay under this title could and should raise for future study: the restoration and constitution of patriarchates; a more effective sectioning off within papal primacy of those administrative obligations that follow upon being patriarch of the West and that, consequently, pertain uniquely to the Western Church; the nature and teaching power of episcopal conferences; the promise and full realization of the potentiality of the synod of bishops; the relationship between jurisdiction and hierarchical communion; etc. But the limitations of time and space indicate that this essay should content itself with two. Both of these deal with the relationship between the bishop and the local church.

Since *Pastor aeternus,* a governing and acknowledged purpose of the primacy has been to "assert, confirm, and vindicate" the episcopate.[1] This strengthening can, as mentioned above, concentrate upon the college itself; but it can also bear upon the relationship between the individual bishop and his diocese. Several further issues suggest themselves here, but one can select from among them two contemporary practices that bespeak the need for further study: the mode of

---

1. *Pastor aeternus,* chap. 3 (DS 3061); Tanner, *Decrees,* 2:814; *Lumen gentium,* no. 27; Tanner, *Decrees,* 2:871.

appointment of bishops and the translation of bishops from see to see.

Both of these comprehend *theoria* embodied in *praxis*, engaging — at least implicitly — a critically important theology of the union between the local bishop and the Church over which he presides. In the history of the Church, many different practices have obtained in the concrete relationships of the bishop with his diocese, practices bespeaking an understanding of the relationship between a bishop and his people and realized in the protocols that govern both appointment of bishops and their translation from see to see.

Appointment of Bishops

By the third century, the selection of bishops was shared in a vital and significant way by three parties: the laity of the local church, the clergy of the local church, and the bishops of the region. This was done in different manners, but all three components were present and active within the election. In the *Apostolic Tradition,* for example, Hippolytus insists that the bishop is to be chosen by all of the people (ὑπὸ παντὸς τοῦ λαοῦ) and that this selection is to be approved by the assembled bishop and presbyters.[2] There is no need to rehearse what has happened since those days. In the East, this suffrage was gradually subsumed by the body of provincial bishops.

> In the West...the limitation of popular suffrage, even in theory, did not take place until a much later period. Evidence for the continued use and acceptance of the older system of episcopal appointment during the fourth and fifth centuries

2. Hippolytus of Rome, *The Treatise on the Apostolic Tradition,* ed. Gregory Dix and Henry Chadwick, 2d rev. ed. (London: Alban Press, 1992), 2:1–2, 2–3.

is provided by Pope Siricius, St. Jerome, Rufinus's account of the election of St. Ambrose, Pope Celestine, and Pope Leo.[3]

William Henn has repeatedly pointed out that the purpose of the great struggle between Gregory VII and Henry IV was not to transfer the power to appoint bishops from secular lords to the primacy — even the *Dictatus papae* does not speak of the papal power or right to appoint bishops — but to "win the freedom of the local churches in selecting their bishops."[4] And he summarizes the history of the Church in this matter: "It would seem that the selection of local bishops was never proposed as a necessary aspect of the primatial ministry as such. The predominant practice of the Church, not only in the first millennium, but even in much of the second seems to suggest otherwise."[5]

To understand the present settlement, one must trace out its complicated development over these centuries as a struggle to secure the unity and freedom of the Church, especially as the Church confronted the rising power of massive

3. Hamilton Hess, *The Canons of the Council of Sardica: A Landmark in the Early Development of Canon Law* (Oxford: Clarendon, 1958), 90–93. For the individual references, see 93 nn. 1–5. The following pages are much in debt to Professor Hess, and in some sentences little more than a paraphrase.

4. William Henn, O.F.M. Cap., "Historical-Theological Synthesis of the Relation between Primacy and Episcopacy during the Second Millennium," *Il primato del successore de Pietro: Atti del simposio teologico, Roma, dicembre 1996* (Vatican City: Libreria Editrice Vaticana, 1997), 225. Henn's conclusion: "The Gregorian reform suggests that the primacy has a responsibility and a right to promote the freedom of local churches in selecting bishops. Thus, the practice of the pope selecting bishops for local churches would not follow from the Gregorian reform but rather would seem to run counter to it." Klaus Schatz, in tracing out this history, agrees with this judgment, speaking of a "papal centralism [that] appeared to be a complete reversal of the Gregorian reforms" (*Papal Primacy: From Its Origins to the Present,* trans. John A. Otto and Linda M. Maloney [Collegeville, Minn.: Liturgical Press, 1996], 97).

5. Henn, "Historical-Theological Synthesis," 226.

nation-states and totalitarian ideologies. The steady use of its authority has enabled the primacy to guarantee for the Church today an independence in the selection of its bishops, an independence it had not enjoyed for many centuries. Perhaps this very independence can now allow the Church to retrieve another element from its tradition, as it has retrieved the notion of *communio,* and restore to the local church a decisive voice in the selection of its bishop. The current highly centralized procedures of the Apostolic See in the selection of bishops might well be seen as a substitutional use of its authority necessitated by the social and political pressures of these past centuries. Would another settlement now strengthen the unity between the bishop and his diocese and reflect the doctrine of the Church on this unity more accurately? For the manner of appointing bishops cannot be reduced to simply Church discipline and practice; it involves a profound understanding of the nature of the diocesan bishop and his union with his people. However one resolves this question, the selection of bishops seems to be an issue that touches directly upon the theological understanding of the character of the diocesan bishop and bears "with particular importance and urgency upon the reflection of the contemporary church."[6]

Today the laity and the local clergy perceive that they possess very little, if any, influence upon the selection of their bishops. Even the bishops of the region are said to have lost effective voice as the selection of the local bishop has been subsumed by the primacy. In a lecture delivered at Oxford University on June 29, 1996, Archbishop John R. Quinn, the former Archbishop of San Francisco, indicated that this process has been centralized into the care of very few, all connected with the papal Curia:

---

6. See page 13 of this essay.

> The nuncio's judgment is generally thought to have the greatest weight, more than that of the local episcopate.... It is not uncommon for bishops of a province to discover that no candidate they proposed has been accepted for approval. On the other hand, it may happen that candidates whom bishops do not approve at all may be appointed.... Under the existing policy, collegiality in the appointment of bishops consists largely in offering bishops an opportunity to make suggestions. But the real decisions are made at other levels: the nuncio, the Congregation of Bishops, the Secretariat of State.

Much more experience than this author possesses would be necessary to determine how accurately this reflects the situation throughout the worldwide Church. It is certainly true that one hears it continually both in the United States and in many countries throughout the world.

There is something paradoxical here: the movement of contemporary world culture is very much in the direction of that widespread inclusion and participative responsibility which characterized the selection of bishops in the early Church; but, in its very desire to insure the independence of the Church, the present practice of the Roman Catholic Church has come to reflect much more the centralizing dynamic of the Roman Empire, which the Church at the time rejected for its own practice. This raises a question that can be framed in many different ways: is the union between the bishop and the local church such that the local church has a right to a decisive voice in the selection of its bishop, not the total voice, but a voice — a right that should only be abrogated in exceptional circumstances? If one does not wish to use "rights language," the question can be framed: should a local church normally be one of the determinators of who will be its bishop? The purpose of this essay is not to argue an answer to that question, but to indicate an area that requires theological inquiry.

Whatever one says about the appropriateness of previous settlements in the selection of bishops and, indeed, of their historical necessity, the very sober question of Archbishop Quinn opens up an area that requires further study:

> Honest, fraternal dialogue compels me to raise the question whether the time has not come to make some modifications in this procedure so that the local churches really have a significant and truly substantive role in the appointment of bishops. In light of the decrees of the Vatican Council itself, the participation of the local churches in this process cannot properly be confined merely to the participation of bishops, but must include a meaningful and responsible role for priests, lay persons and religious.[7]

Whatever modifications are to be made in this matter must both reflect and strengthen the unity of the bishop with his people, and especially with his clergy. Were the primacy to take the lead in such a reform, it would resume in a very different way the Gregorian concern for the freedom of the local church.

The Translation of Bishops

In the early Church, the union between the bishop and his local church was understood as far more profound than that of jurisdiction and even of sacramental functions. Hamilton Hess summarizes it in this way: The election of the bishop "by an almost independent Christian community and his essential fatherhood among his people, as standing in place of Christ Himself, appear to have given rise to the concept of a mystical union existing between the bishop and

---

7. John R. Quinn, "The Claims of the Primacy and the Costly Call to Unity," a lecture on the occasion of the centennial of Campion Hall (June 29, 1996), *Origins* 26, no. 8 (July 18, 1996): 124.

his see which was expressed as being akin to the marriage bond."[8] This theological vision founded the repeated condemnations of the movement of a bishop from see to see, a prohibition that constituted canon 15 of Nicea, canon 5 of Chalcedon, as well as those of many regional councils. The Council of Alexandria (338) even called such a translated bishop an adulterer, while a synod of Carthage (397) classified the translation of bishops "with the forbidden practices of rebaptism and reordination."[9] Translation was not considered simply a matter of canonical discipline. The legislation involved an implicit theology of the relationship of a bishop with his see and the sacredness and inviolability of their union. Interestingly enough, the prohibition against translation was followed with particular fidelity in the West.

The theological vision of the mystical union between the bishop and his diocese reinforced a moral and practical concern. The translation of bishops from one see to another was often motivated by ambition and driven by the will-to-power. Sarcastically, the first canon of the Council of Sardica (342) noted: "Almost no bishop is found who will move from a large city to a small one.... Whence it appears that they are inflamed by the heat of avarice to serve ambition." Pope Julius alludes to the same when he writes:

> If therefore you truly consider the honor due to all bishops to be the same and equal, and, as you write, do not measure the dignity of a bishop by the greatness of his city; it is fitting that he who has been established in a small city should remain there... and not move to another not entrusted to him, that by despising that which he was given by God [τῆς μὲν παρὰ θεοῦ δοθείσης] he should foolishly hope for the approbation of men."[10]

---

8. Hess, *The Canons of the Council of Sardica*, 71.
9. Hess, *The Canons of the Council of Sardica*, 72.
10. Hess, *The Canons of the Council of Sardica*, 76–77.

This recognition of the divine action in the entrustment of a diocese to a bishop and of the disintegration of this realization by the drive for another and better diocese did not lay down an absolute prohibition from which there were no exceptions possible. By synodal action and as an exceptional response to the needs of the Church or by divine revelation(!), a bishop from one see could be appointed to another see.[11] But the rarity of this occurrence effectively removed the use of a smaller diocese as a stepping stone to a bigger diocese and with this prohibition offered a significant check to ecclesiastical ambition.

Karl Baus summarized the persuasions and the development in this history during the early centuries in the Church:

> The unlimited duty of caring for his community also justified the prohibition to transfer a bishop to another see, which was motivated by patristic theology with the idea of a mystical marriage between bishop and local church, to be terminated only by death. In the course of the fourth century this prohibition, despite strict sanctions such as deposition and excommunication, was again and again disregarded and in the East often led to serious conflicts. From the beginning of the fifth century there appeared an easing of the prohibition, since reasons for exceptions were recognized — rejection of a new bishop by the community, prohibition of entering upon the office by the secular power, pastoral necessity. The

---

11. See Hess, *The Canons of the Council of Sardica*, for the strictness of the West and the greater flexibility in the East when "the Church as a whole would benefit by the transfer of a bishop or cleric from one church to another" (71–72). This latter he styles "the considered transferal of a bishop by synodical action," as opposed to those "for personal or party gain" (76). One will find the early legislation forbidding the translation of bishops in the Council of Arles (314), canon 2; Council of Nicea (325), canon 15; Council of Antioch (c. 328), canon 21; Apostolic Canons, canon 14; Council of Sardica (343), canons 1, 2, 15, 16, 19. See Tanner, *Decrees*, 1:95 n. 1.

provincial synod had to consider whether deposition was to be decreed because of serious lapses, but against its verdict the one concerned had the right to appeal to Rome, which inquired whether the case was to be taken up at another synod.[12]

The strength and seriousness of this prohibition lay behind some of the most spectacular moments in the early Church: Gregory of Nazianzus was forced to resign the see of Constantinople because of his previous consecration for Sasima, a resignation demanded by Pope Damasus among others, citing canon 15 of Nicea.[13] Some four centuries later, in January 897, Pope Stephen VI had the corpse of his predecessor, Formosus, disinterred and brought before a special synod, which declared his election to Rome null, purporting to justify this bizarre political action by citing his previous occupancy of the see of Porto.[14] A saner and more significant indication of Rome's profound reverence for the conciliar prohibition against the translation of bishops lies with its consistent refusal during virtually the entire first millennium to elect as bishop of Rome anyone who had been or was already bishop of another see. The first departure from this practice occurred in the election of Marinus I in 882.

Would it be true to assert that what the early Church for centuries condemned is now accepted practice in the Roman Catholic Church today? There is nothing intrinsic to papal primacy that demands such a diminishment

---

12. Karl Baus, "Inner Life of the Church between Nicea and Chalcedon," in *History of the Church*, ed. Hubert Jedin and John Dolan (New York: Seabury Press, 1980), 2:232.

13. W. H. C. Frend, *The Early Church* (Philadelphia: Fortress Press, 1965), 174–76.

14. Eugen Ewig, "The Western Church from the Death of Louis the Pious to the End of the Carolingian Period," in *History of the Church*, 3:155–56.

of the stable relationship between a local bishop and his people, and it effectively reduces the bond between them. Perhaps this is another area that can be suggested for further study.

•

In summary: For centuries in the early Church, "the relationship of a bishop to his church was seen as a spiritual marriage." This theological understanding carried with it two implications: (*a*) "like the assent of the partners in a marriage, the [local] church's 'yes' must be freely given"; (*b*) the translation of a bishop to another see was prohibited except in very rare cases.[15] There were canons that specified the first and prohibited the second. This doctrine of the almost mystical unity between the bishop and his diocese deserves additional study in the contemporary Church.

Two questions arise in this context: whether the present settlement actually detracts from the full vigor of the episcopate and whether papal restoration of ancient legislation on the selection of bishops and their stability within their sees could contribute significantly to the strengthening of the episcopate and the local churches today. Could the Apostolic See further effectively its responsibilities simply by restoring what has been taken from the local churches over the centuries? This would be to retrieve in a very different way that papal leadership whose bent was the strength and freedom of the local church. Neither problem is an easy one to resolve, but both merit serious study and each touches upon both components of this essay.

For finally, the primacy is vital to the degree that the episcopate is strengthened and united. It is not a weak episcopate

---

15. Schatz, *Papal Primacy*, 97–98.

that indicates a powerful primacy; it is a strong episcopate. So also the episcopate is vital to the degree that the people of God it is to serve are actualized and local churches are brought into the communion and the freedom that is their sacramental heritage.

OF RELATED INTEREST

Phyllis Zagano & Terrence W. Tilley, Editors

THE EXERCISE OF THE PRIMACY
Continuing the Dialogue

Archbishop Quinn's remarkable Oxford lecture on the relationship between the Pope and the bishops, with responses by leading scholars.

In June 1996, **Archbishop John Quinn** delivered a lecture at Campion Hall at Oxford on the relationship between the Pope and the bishops, offering both an acute assessment of the present situation and bold proposals for reform. In order to carry forward the discussion occasioned by Archbishop Quinn's lecture, this volume presents the text of the Oxford lecture as well as responses by five prominent Catholic thinkers who examine the issues raised from a variety of perspectives:

R. Scott Appleby
Elizabeth A. Johnson
John F. Kane
Thomas P. Rausch
Wendy M. Wright

0-8245-1744-X; $14.95 paperback

Please support your local bookstore, or call 1-800-395-0690.
For a free catalog, please write us at
THE CROSSROAD PUBLISHING COMPANY
370 LEXINGTON AVENUE, NEW YORK, NY 10017

We hope you enjoyed Papal Primacy and the Episcopate.
Thank you for reading it.

crossroad
herder